Get Your Worth

Land Your Dream Job With 100+ Simple Strategies

Dr. Jasper Kim

Table Of Contents

Introduction

Get Your Worth: Land Your Dream Job With 100+ Simple Strategies empowers you with simple strategies for job negotiation success. What magic words are best for a job negotiation? What last question should you ask at the end of your job negotiation? How do you know when to say no to a job offer? What nonverbals make you appear more confident? And how do you counter biases during the job interview process?

Get Your Worth is purposefully simple and specific. It provides actionable details, exact examples and in-the-moment dialogues that go beyond broad and sweeping platitudes, such as "be more confident" or "do your research." This book is your masterclass guide to becoming a savvy job negotiator and beyond.

With ***Get Your Worth***, you'll be a force inside and outside the interview room. Each simple strategy will get you one step closer to your dream job offer. Through the 100+ simple strategies shared in this book, you'll learn how to:

* **Master the art of persuasion for job negotiations:** Learn how to use your words and body language to create a powerful first impression and wield invisible influence and sway on the people who hire you

* **Unleash your inner confidence:** Discover the secrets to project confidence and self-assurance, even when you're feeling nervous or unsure of yourself

* **Develop winning job negotiation strategies:** Learn how to research your worth, identify your negotiation goals and develop an action-based plan that will help you achieve your goals based on cutting-edge scientific studies

* **Respond and reflect common job negotiation tactics:** Arm yourself with the knowledge you need to recognize and counter common negotiation tactics, such as lowball offers, dirty tactics and emotional appeals

* **Close the deal to land your dream job:** Learn how to negotiate final terms, sign the offer, and walk away with the job offer you deserve.

With these powerful 100+ simple strategies that have proven to work, you'll be able to transform yourself into a negotiation ninja, capable of securing the salary, benefits and respect you deserve. Ditch the fear and embrace the power of controlling your destiny by asserting yourself and what you want in your next job negotiation. Through this book, you'll be unstoppable in the job market — to land your dream job — and get your worth.

In ***Get Your Worth: Land Your Dream Job With 100+ Simple Strategies***, you'll learn:

* The psychology of **persuasion**

* How to read people's **body language**

* How to project **confidence**

* How to **know your worth**

* Know when to **say no and walkaway**

* How to identify your **negotiation goals**

* How to create a winning **negotiation strategy**

* Develop mental models through knowing the right **mindset and strategies**

* How to respond to common negotiation tactics and **dirty tactics**

* Know when and how to **ask for more**

* How to close and **seal the deal**

This book is purposefully designed for people of all backgrounds, industries and skillsets based on my experience teaching negotiations at UC Berkeley, University of Oxford and other leading institutions. The 100+ simple strategies in this book represent a culmination of over two decades of research augmented by my experience interviewing and coaching over 2,000 working professionals and students for positions and opportunities worldwide.

Know that even taking action on just one of the 100+ simple strategies in this book will give you a competitive edge over other Job Candidates — catapulting your chances for success and landing your dream job.

You deserve to get what you're worth. By choosing ***Get Your Worth: Land Your Dream Job With 100+ Simple Strategies***, you've taken the important first step to transform yourself into a powerful, principled and persuasive negotiator to land your dream job.

Dr. Jasper Kim

Berkeley, California

Author's Note:

The 100+ simple strategies in this book are often written in the context of landing an initial job offer, but importantly, these same simple strategies can also empower you to negotiate your worth in other career-related contexts (pay raise, promotion, corner office and better or equal treatment from your boss or manager, just to name a few). Also, the terms "you," "job candidate," "employee," and "interviewee" are generally used interchangeably, as are the terms "organization," "firm," "recruiter," "employer," "manager" and "interviewer." For clarity, this book is not a "how to" for writing cover letters or resumes (CVs) or a "step-by-step guide" for every facet of the job application process. This book is instead a curated collection of 100+ simple strategies for certain, but not all, sectors and job seekers various stages of the job application process to maximize your chance of success.

Part 1: Before The Job Interview

1. Know Your Breaking Point

Simple Strategy

How do you know if you should say yes or no to a job offer? As a Job Candidate, you should first determine — before your job negotiation — your exact minimum breaking point for your salary (as a Recruiter, you would frame it as an exact *maximum* salary amount). What amount would be so extreme for you or the Recruiter to say no? This may seem quite basic but that's the point. This is because thinking about breaking points is often overlooked or tossed aside to the last minute, which often leads to non-optimal outcomes. The formal term for your breaking point is Reservation Point (RP). Knowing your Reservation Point is crucial for effective negotiation because it serves as a reference point for evaluating job offers. It helps you establish boundaries, avoid making impulsive decisions and further ensures that you know when to walk away or say yes to a job offer.

Simple Example

You decide your Reservation Point (RP) (Breaking Point) Salary is $90,000

Hiring Manager: I'm prepared to offer you $85,000 for this position.

You: I appreciate the offer very much. Having said this, based on my research and experience, I believe a salary closer to $99,000 would be more appropriate.

Hiring Manager: I understand your perspective. However, our budget for this position is $85,000. Is there anything else we can do to make the offer more attractive?

You: I appreciate the question. I'm open to discussing additional benefits, such as a signing bonus or more vacation time. Could we discuss potential ways to incorporate both elements into the offer?

Hiring Manager: We may be able to accommodate your request, given your exceptional expertise and skills. Based on what we've discussed, I'm prepared to offer you a revised package that includes a salary of $90,000 plus a $5,000 signing bonus and two more days of vacation days for the first year.

You: I appreciate your flexibility. I think that's very reasonable. I'd be prepared to accept your offer based on those terms.

2. Know Your Ideal Deal

Simple Strategy

Do you know your ideal and specific salary bullseye point? This is known as your Aspiration Point (AP). It represents a best-case scenario and serves as a benchmark for evaluating job offers and making decisions. As a rough analogy, if you were playing darts, think of your Aspiration Point (AP) as your bullseye (ideal point) and your Reservation Point (acceptable breaking point) as the entire dartboard. Your AP provides a constant reminder of your specific target salary throughout the job negotiation process to ensure you get your worth. Studies show that sales teams that focus on a specific Aspiration Point (bullseye target) were more successful than compared to those that didn't focus on an AP. The takeaway: to get what you want in a job negotiation, you must first know exactly what you want.

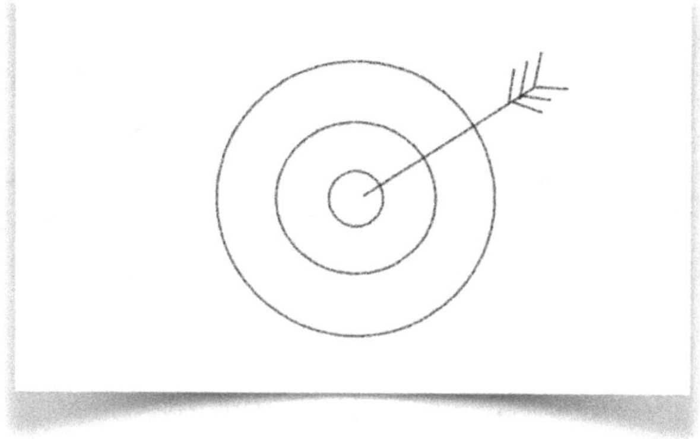

Simple Example

You decide:

* *Your Aspiration Point (AP) (Ideal) Salary is $155,000*
* *Your Reservation Point (RP) (Minimum) Salary is $150,000*

Hiring Manager: I'd like to offer you $145,000 for your salary increase. This is $5,000 more a year than you're currently making.

You: Unfortunately, that figure is not something I'm able to accept in its current form. What I can accept, based on my performance and KPIs (Key Performance Indicators), is a salary of $157,000.

Hiring Manager: How about we meet in the middle at $151,000?

You: How about we meet in the middle, plus just $4,000 more for my first year salary, which can be extended based on meeting my KPIs?

Hiring Manager: Why don't we do this: $151,000 plus $4,000 more in stock options based on meeting your KPIs?

You: I think we have an agreement.

3. What's Your Yes Zone?

Simple Strategy

Thinking only about your salary expectations is just one piece of your job negotiation strategy. You also need to think about your potential employer's salary expectations. It takes two to tango, especially in a job negotiation. To get to the Yes Zone, make estimates of each of your walkaway points. For you (the Job Candidate), this is your Breaking Point (Reservation Point), covered earlier, which in this case is your *minimum* (salary). But remember: the Firm also has a Breaking Point, which is their *maximum* (salary). The overlap and common ground for both sides is the overall Yes Zone (or more formally, ZOPA, the Zone of Possible Agreements) — this is the "win-win" zone — where both sides are better off saying yes than no to the offer at play. If an offer is given to you that's in your ZOPA, it's one important factor that can pivot you towards saying yes.

Simple Example

Identifying the Zone of Possible Agreement (ZOPA):

* **Your Reservation Point** is 90,000 (minimum breaking point)

* **Company's Reservation Point** is $100,000 (maximum breaking point)

* **ZOPA** falls between $90,000 and $100,000 (Yes Zone, where you should consider saying yes to a job offer)

4. Should You Cooperate Or Compete?

Simple Strategy

One strategic question underlying negotiations is whether you should cooperate or compete with your counterparty. This is an academic area known as Prisoner's Dilemma (PD), where two players must decide whether to cooperate or not. Research findings show that in a one-time (non-iterated) meeting, the most effective PD strategy is to compete (or betray), which means get as much as you can, at the potential expense of the relationship. But with more than one (iterated) interaction, the most effective PD strategy is a mirroring strategy, known as Tit-for-Tat (TfT; where you cooperate if the other side cooperates, but you compete if the other side competes).

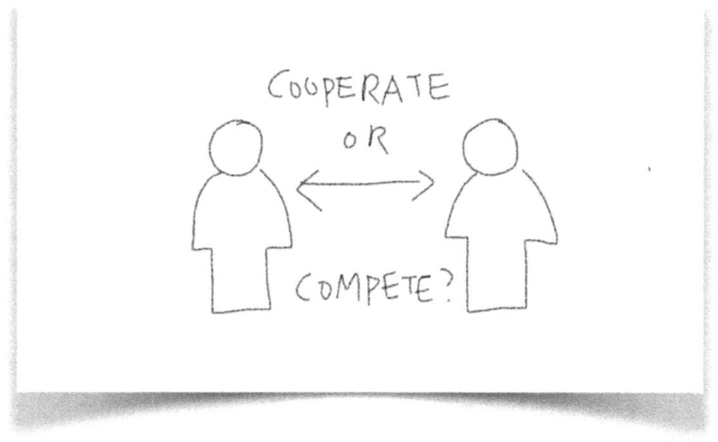

Simple Example

Sarah, a talented software engineer, is interviewing with a promising startup. The company, Alpha Inc., offers an exciting project and a positive work culture, but the initial salary offer falls short of Sarah's expectations. This creates a negotiation scenario similar to the prisoner's dilemma.

* **The Options:**
- **Accept (Cooperate):** Sarah accepts the initial offer to secure the job and the company gains a valuable employee. (Payoff: Moderate satisfaction for both)
- **Negotiate (Compete):** Sarah pushes for a higher salary, potentially alienating the company but possibly achieving a better outcome. (Payoff: High for Sarah if successful, low if rejected; Low for Alpha if Sarah leaves, moderate if Sarah accepts a raise)

* **The Dilemma:**
- Sarah fears that being too demanding (compete) might lead Alpha to withdraw the offer altogether. On the other hand, accepting the lower offer (cooperate) means settling for less than her worth.

* **Possible Strategies:**
- **Prepare strong arguments for a higher salary:** Research market rates, highlight her skills and experience, and showcase her enthusiasm for the project.

- **Be open to compromise:** Express her desire to work at Alpha and be willing to negotiate within a reasonable range.

- **Gauge Alpha's response:** Look for cues in their communication about their budget flexibility and their interest in Sarah's skills.

By focusing on open communication and building rapport, Sarah and Alpha can move away from a purely self-interested approach. By demonstrating her value and understanding Alpha's needs, Sarah can increase the chances of a win-win outcome (cooperate-cooperate).

5. Fight For Your Value

Simple Strategy

Knowing your value lets you know what you bring to the table. Incorporating transaction lists to show your value is an approach advocated by many firms from McKinsey & Company to Accenture. Calculate your value using both words *and* numbers. Both should tell the same story — that you're valuable — and should thus be a priority hire. So, create a Transactions List section in your resume (CV), listing the transaction description, counterparty, specific duties and the overall monetary value associated with the transaction, case or client (feel free to adapt and tweak this as needed for your industry or sector).

Simple Example

- Your Resume (CV)

Transaction List

Transaction Description: Structuring of a tax-efficient booking vehicle for domestic assets

Counterparty: Offshore institutional client

Tasks and Duties: Liaised with tax and legal counsel to structure tax-efficient booking vehicle strategic options. Served as transactor (hub) within the Firm between the business (trading) and tax/legal teams

Transaction Value: $2,500,000 (in terms of gross tax savings)

6. Be Likable Using Similarities

Simple Strategy

We're our own biggest fans. But we can be judgey about other people. Some attribute this to self-preservation or even narcissism. Some would say the two are one in the same. Whichever is the case, try to be as similar as possible to the person or group hiring you. This strategy of getting the hiring side to see themselves in you is known as Liking Theory. It says that we like people who give us (genuine) compliments. We also like people who agree with us. And finally, we like people who are similar to us. Similarities, big and small, often correlate with likability. And the more likable we seem in the job negotiation, the higher the chance that you'll be given a job offer. Why so? Because we appear similar enough to the person hiring us. Remember: people love themselves.

Simple Example

- **Before your job interview:** try to find at least three specific similarities you have with your potential job interviewer. You can try looking at LinkedIn, your potential employer's website and publicly available sources

- **During your job interview:** as you greet your potential job interviewer, mention similarities, professional or personal. For example, you can say,"I noticed from the Firm's website that you studied overseas at Oxford. So did I! What a small world!"

7. When To Frame As A Gain

Simple Strategy

You've probably heard the aphorism that you can get the answer you want by the way you ask the question. This means getting the answer you want is a frame game. Here's a case in point based on the Nobel Laureate, Daniel Kahneman. If you want the Job Interviewer to be *risk-averse*, frame things as a gain (a win). This will be useful if you believe that the Recruiter will view your qualifications and background as the more traditional or safer option.

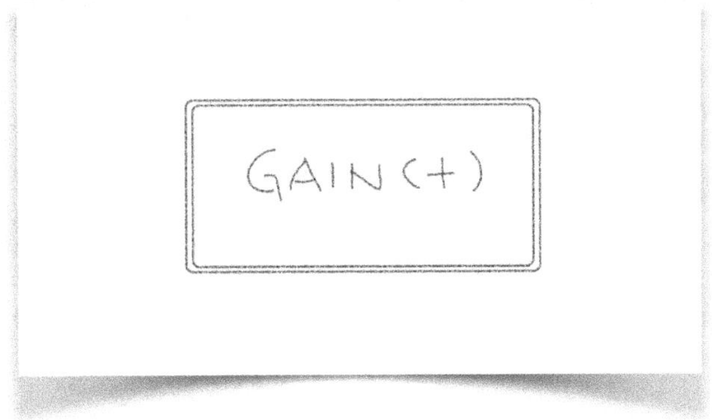

Simple Example

Let's say you have a well-pedigreed background that would meet the job specifications (which would also make the Firm appear both competent and prestigious).

Managing Partner: It certainly seems that your academic credentials would make an ideal fit with our Firm. We've hired from your prestigious alma mater for decades and have always been very pleased with whom we've hired.

You: I'm truly flattered. Receiving your offer is both appreciated and humbling. As you're probably already aware, graduates from my alma mater are exceptionally hard working, and seem to flourish and prosper at your Firm. It's a beneficial and *safe* bet for everyone.

8. When To Frame As A Loss

Simple Strategy

In contrast to the previous strategy, if you want the Recruiter to be *risk-taking*, frame the notion of *not* hiring you in terms of a *loss*. It turns out that humans, including Recruiters, hate losses. Even the thought of a loss triggers a similar emotional response in the brain to actual physical pain. If people were perfectly rational decision-makers, we would hate losses as much as we love gains. But it turns out, as supported by several studies, we hate losses *twice as much* as we love gains. In other words, the love-hate, win-loss relationship tilts very much towards hating losses over loving gains. This is what's known as Loss Aversion Theory (LAT).

Simple Example

Let's say that you don't have a so-called "elite" pedigree. Instead, you are a graduate from a mid-tier large state university. You have some work experience, but not at white shoe institutions. However, you've taught yourself how to code during the weekends and off hours.

Recruiter: After reviewing your resume (CV), I'm not sure if your non-traditional background would make sense for the position.

You: I know I don't exactly have the well-worn background you may be seeking from an institution like Stanford or Google in my resume (CV). But what I have is grit. What I also have is a thirst for knowledge and getting better every single day. You can teach concepts, but you can't teach grit and the need to succeed. Which is why *not* hiring me will be a huge *loss* for your Firm.

9. Use The Positivity Principle

Simple Strategy

You may have heard the song, "Don't worry, be happy." For an interview setting, the rebranded working title would be, "Don't worry, be *positive*." Research shows that having a positive mindset and persona is highly helpful. Much like volleying back a tennis ball to your sender, those who observe you showcasing a positive mindset will also think of you more positively. The opposite also holds true. If you display a negative mindset and persona, people will tend to view you more negatively. So, the strategy is to turn that frowny mindset upside down. Become that person who sees things from a rose-tinted, glass half-full perspective. Remember the mantra: mind over matter. Your mindset controls your image. And in a job interview context, image is (almost) everything. So go ahead and display energetic body language. Describe things as opportunities, not problems. Studies also suggest that positive people tend to find greater opportunities. When salespeople believed that they would make a particular sale, they were 55% more successful than their pessimistic counterparts. Some would call this luck. But based on scientific studies, luck is not only the residue of preparation — it can also be created by being positive.

Simple Example

Recruiter: It seems that you quit your job at Firm X after just three months. Do you just lose interest quickly or did your job at Firm X not meet your expectations?

You: Working at Firm X was an amazing experience! I met so many great people while working there. Honestly, I originally intended to work there for quite a while, but then a once-in-a-lifetime opportunity presented itself to learn how to code. It's always been my dream to create, and learning to create by coding has turned out to be an absolutely perfect fit for me. It also led me to the amazing opportunity of speaking with you and your coding team here today.

10. Anchor Away

Simple Strategy

People are often surreptitiously and subtly swayed. One way to subtly sway is through Anchoring. Anchoring involves asking questions or making statements anchored to a specific number or point. Based on several studies, the specific number or point doesn't even have to be factually correct or related to the question or statement being made. What's the end result of Anchoring? If asked a question with a specific anchor (reference point), people tend to give an answer that's pretty close to that anchor.

Simple Example

Recruiter: So, let's talk numbers. Would a salary of $92,000 work for you?

You: That's an interesting starting salary figure. Could we discuss ways to increase the number to $100,000?

Recruiter: The Firm prefers a figure near $92,000. But given your background, I can go up to $95,000.

You: I appreciate the upward movement from your starting number of $92,000. I think we're very close to an agreeable number.

11. Find Your Why

Simple Strategy

One negotiation model taught in business schools is known as the Integrative Bargaining Model (IBM). It's an aspirational model that aims to cooperate, rather than compete, with negotiation counterparties. One feature of Integrative Bargaining is to find Shared Interests. Interests are *why* you and the Recruiter want a particular thing. It's often a story, feeling or other invisible influencer that's often left unsaid, such as pride, guilt or greed. (This contrasts from Positions seen in a Positional Bargaining Model. A Position is *what* the parties want, such as price, quantity or time in a dealmaking situation.) The takeaway: explore Shared Interests (not Positions) since Shared Interests act as magnetizing forces to get to yes.

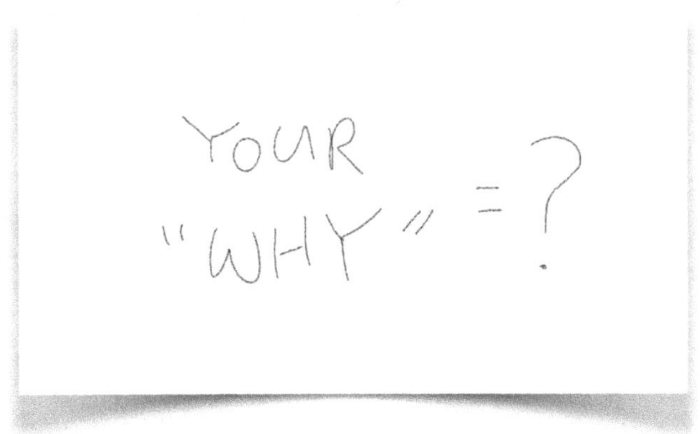

Simple Example

Recruiter: I think $100,000 is the most that we can offer you. (*Recruiter's "Position"*)

You: That's an understandable starting number. Correct me if I'm wrong, but I'm assuming that mitigating risk and costs is an Interest for you and the Firm. Based on this Shared Interest, how about I forgo the *guaranteed* bonus, and we replace it with a *performance-based* bonus? This way the Firm pays me nothing if I don't meet or exceed expectations. In this deal, you and the Firm only pay for success, which is something both of us share (*as a Shared Interest*).

12. Use Emotional IQ+

Simple Strategy

If you were a Hollywood blockbuster movie director, you would pay particular focus on your movie's opening and closing scenes. Think of Star Wars, James Bond or any Marvel movie where the dramatic opening sequence instantly captures your attention. This is done by grabbing your *emotional attention.* Fear, love, hate, shock and hope are visceral examples of emotions that carry over to subsequent sequences of the movie, before a cinematic crescendo culminates into the movie's climax. From Hollywood movies — to punchy and emotionally-drenched commercials — your emotional attention is being set on fire. The strategy is to focus not so much on how the movie will make you *think*, but how the movie will make you *feel.* This emotional residue, if executed well, will tend to stick with you and your subsequent view of your cinematic experience. Knowing this is part of your Emotional IQ+ toolbox. Linking emotions to job interviews, if we were perfectly rational decision-makers, we would come to a conclusion to hire or not based purely on logical reasons. But in reality, the process is flipped. Studies suggest that we often come to an *emotional* conclusion first and then try to find rational reasons to support it. For example, an interviewer may be more likely to hire a Job Candidate they feel comfortable with, even if that person isn't the most qualified. Given such potential pitfalls, in your job interview, the strategy is to ask yourself *before* the job negotiation, "What do I want the recruiter to *feel* about me?"

Simple Example

Recruiter: I see that you took an extra year to finish your graduate studies. This is a bit concerning, since we're an organization of high achievers. If you don't mind me asking, what exactly was the reason for this delay?

You: I certainly aimed to complete my graduate degree within two years in a more traditional path. However, as a single working mother raising a young child, I made the difficult decision to take a nontraditional path and work extra hours based on financial considerations to support my family. Fortunately, I was able to switch my student status to part-time and still complete the program relatively quickly given my unique circumstances.

Recruiter: Thank you for sharing that information. As a parent myself, I'm genuinely impressed by what you've accomplished under such challenging conditions. I truly *feel* like our Firm needs more people like you, who have faced real world daunting challenges and have come out a stronger and better person as a result of it.

13. Your Elevator Pitch Should Be Pitch Perfect

42

Simple Strategy

People are busy — particularly people who hire Job Candidates. Because of hectic schedules, people sometimes don't have all the time in the world to be fully aware of all your amazing accomplishments. Honestly, some may only have the time to skim over your cover letter and resume (CV) in a few short minutes right before interviewing you, despite the fact that you may have spent days or weeks editing every last letter and comma. Time is money, or at least opportunity cost. Which is why you should create a short and catchy elevator pitch that succinctly and persuasively combines both your cover letter and resume (CV). To do this, create a Top 5 list of buzzwords most important and relevant to the job description. Then use active verbs and short punchy sentences to connect the buzzwords. According to the *Harvard Business Review*, the key elements of a great pitch or presentation includes having a clear purpose, conveying a compelling story and utilizing effective visuals. Much like in action movies, make your initial impression count. People pay more attention to what they see or read first, known as the *primacy effect*. So particularly focus on the first words of your pitch — this is when your audience is paying the most attention — albeit in an elevator or any other elevated situation.

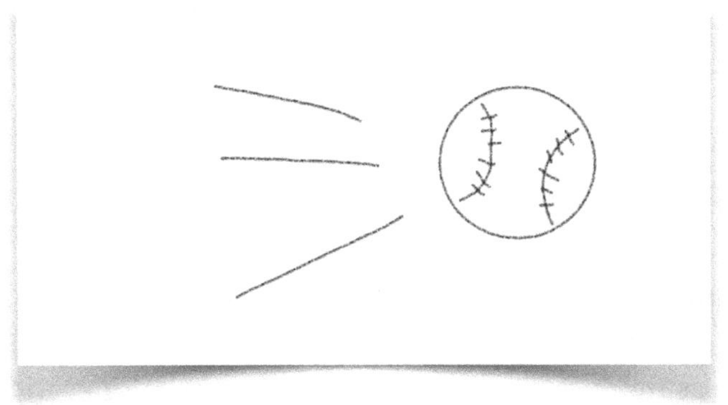

Simple Example

You: Hi, I'm Maya, a freelance writer with a passion for crafting compelling content that engages readers and drives results. I specialize in a variety of platforms, including websites, blogs, social media and marketing materials. Whether you need SEO-optimized (Search Engine Optimization) blog posts, engaging social media captions or persuasive email campaigns, I'm here to help you achieve your content marketing goals!

14. Use Specific Words (From The Job Description)

Simple Strategy

Recruiters and HR personnel can instantly spot a one-size-fits-all, copy-and-paste resume (CV) and/or cover letter. This is known as the "pray and spray" tactic. You may think, "Hey, my background generally covers the job description enough." But the key term that doesn't help you is "generally." Instead, be a heat-seeking guided missile that signals you know what the job requires (the Demand Side), and also that your unique and specific set of skills and experience are perfectly matched for the job (the Supply Side). The strategy here is to mirror keywords from the job description to your cover letter and resume (CV). While doing this, make sure to customize your experience, courses and other accomplishments to those most similar to the job description. When using online resumes (CVs), use online resume (CV) scanner apps (Jobscan and others), where your job description matches should be between 60 to 85 percent. These strategies will help maximize the chance to get to yes, whether it's an algorithm or an actual human reviewing your submitted job application documents on the other side.

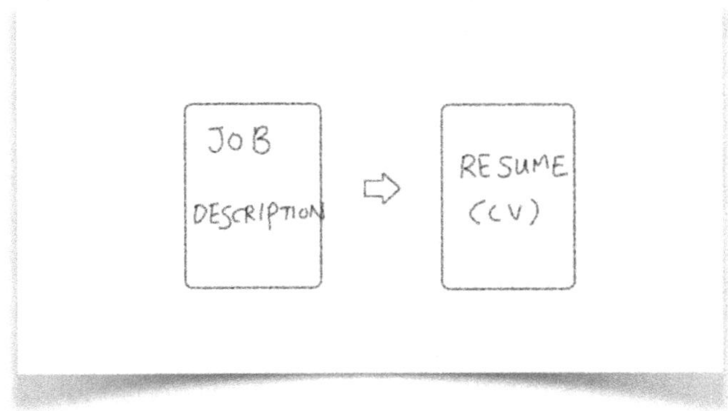

Simple Example

- Job Description

* Experience with animation, motion graphics or 3D modeling software

* Experience shooting video and working with cameras

* Knowledge of specific video formats and compression techniques

* Understanding of copyright law and best practices for using copyrighted material

- Your Resume (CV)

Courses Taken: Animation (Grade: A), 3D Modeling Software (Grade: A+), Intellectual Property and Copyright Law (Grade: A-), Video Digital Editing (Grade: A)

15. Show Your Uniqueness

Simple Strategy

When submitting your cover letter and resume (CV), you have to strike a strategic balance between "fitting in" and "standing out." If you fit in too much, you'll blandly blend into the applicant crowd. Given that only a small fraction of job applicants are contacted for interviews, this shouldn't be your winning move. On the other hand, if your cover letter and resume (CV) stands out too much, it will likely also get passed over for being an out-of-place outlier. So what's the strategic strike zone? One strategy is to mostly conform both to the industry norm, but have splashes of slightly positive individuality in it. It's a bit like adding a splash of color to an otherwise pro forma business suit by wearing a scarf, socks or tie with a slight splash and dash of color.

Simple Example

- **Your Resume (CV)**

Hobbies: Rubik's Cube Competitions, Stand-Up Comedy, DJ for weddings, Rock Climbing, Volunteer Teaching for Underserved Populations and Communities

Accomplishments: MacArthur ("Genius") Grant, Rhodes Scholar, Boston Marathon Finalist, Field Hockey Varsity Team

16. If You've Got It, Flaunt It

Simple Strategy

It's an attention economy. Applying for jobs isn't an effort in humility or subtlety. In today's age, you have to be clear, direct, punchy and persuasive. So, strut your stuff. It's only bragging if you can't back it up. Whatever makes you a high achiever, show the Recruiter and HR team what you've got. From a stellar GPA to a steady stream of increased responsibilities and promotions at work, show your audience that you mean business to get their business.

Simple Example

- Your Resume (CV)

GPA: 3.9 (summa cum laude)

Progressive Promotions / Titles: Analyst (Year 1), Senior Analyst (Year 2), Associate (Year 3)

17. Showcase Your Professional Skills

Simple Strategy

Your skills reflect your value. Skills include those that are computational (Microsoft Office Suite and others), analytical (ability to analyze) and linguistic (proficiency in more than one language). Another useful skill is leadership. Most career arcs are a filtering process. When you first apply for an internship or full-time position, you're competing against many other applicants. When you're promoted, you're the chosen one (over similarly-situated professionals, including peers and competitors). Rising to the top of the pyramid shows determination and a will to make things happen. When considering potential applicants, you can be sure that the applicant with more leadership skills has the greater ROI (Return on Investment) potential from the organization's perspective. Albeit leadership, computational, analytical or language skills, make sure to explicitly list them in your resume (CV) and discuss them during your job interview. By hiring and choosing you over other Job Candidates, the organization is taking a bet on you — and you're also taking a bet on them.

Simple Example

- Your Resume (CV)

Leadership Roles

Student Body President
Co-Captain, Collegiate Lacrosse Team (Division I)
Intern (Year 1), Organizational Leader, CSR Team (Year 2)

18. Stay With Your Strengths

Simple Strategy

Let's face it. A job interview is a potentially stressful situation. You're meeting people you don't know, and these people could be your future bosses. Their interview task is simple: to judge you. This may seem daunting and terrifying, but only if you think of the interview game as only a game of defense — where you're constantly backpedaling trying to defend yourself — against any and all questions coming at you with whatever answers you give in real time. Instead, reframe the interview game as a *game of both offense and defense*. Your strengths are your plays on offense. Write a Top 10 list of your specific strengths. When doing this, think about the following questions: What do you know well? What can you explain well that others would find useful? What's easy for you but hard for other people? What do you do when you're in a flow state? After doing this, when you're in an interview, reframe the interview game to your core Top 10 specific strengths. Do this by not answering the direct question that was asked if it plays to your weakness, but by repivoting and reframing the question to your strengths. Harness your inner politician for strategic success.

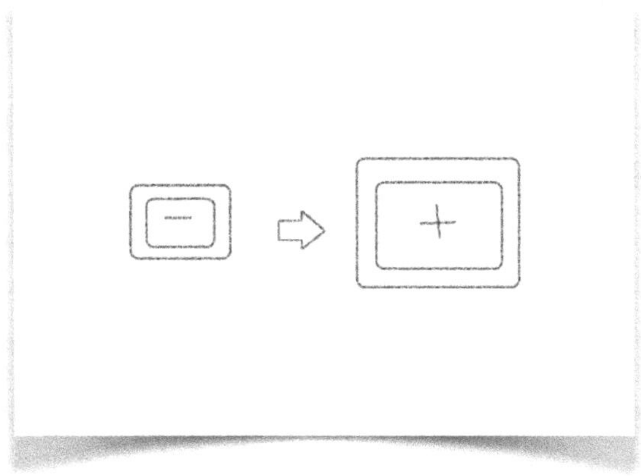

Simple Example

Interviewer: My next interview question is: what are your takeaways from the recent news relating to artificial intelligence (AI)?

You: As a philosophy major, I think this question is profound. The question highlights the importance of ethics pertaining to AI. Specifically, what ethical frameworks — such as utilitarianism, deontology or virtue ethics — should be used to ensure the safety of AI for current and future stakeholders and society? These fundamental philosophical questions are as important now as they ever were in human history.

19. Strike A (Power) Pose

Simple Strategy

You've heard the axion, "Fake it 'til you make it." Similarly, you should "Power Pose 'til you make it." What's a Power Pose and why do it? A Power Pose is a simple two minute purposeful pose that can trigger certain chemical reactions in your brain. There are two types of Power Poses: High Power Poses and Low Power Poses. A High Power Pose involves poses and postures that make yourself larger, such as expanding your body by stretching your body and arms outwards. Studies show that a High Power Pose boosts your confidence (through increased testosterone), while lowering stress levels (through decreased cortisol). A Low Power Pose involves poses and postures that make yourself smaller or submissive, albeit knowingly or unknowingly. The chemical reaction within your brain when entering a Low Power Pose is the polar opposite of a High Power Pose. By entering a Low Power Pose, your confidence collapses (with lower testosterone) and your stress spikes (with higher cortisol). So, your best strategy is to purposely strike a pose — specifically, a High Power Pose — for at least two minutes *before* your job interview. Warning: don't enter into a High Power Pose during the interview itself. Instead, find a secluded and quiet place (even a bathroom stall if this is all that's available) to cognitively convert yourself from a timid mouse (with low confidence and high stress levels) to Mighty Mouse (with great confidence and low stress levels). Power Poses speak louder than words.

Simple Example

High Power Pose (Do This for Two Minutes Just Before Your Interview): Put your hands on your hips while widening your standing position — envision a *specific* dialogue and scene of your successful job interview session.

Low Power Pose (Don't Do This Right Before Your Interview): Crouching with your head down to look at your smartphone while waiting in the hallway for your interview — this is an example of unknowingly entering into a Low Power Pose at possibly the worst time ever (right before job interview showtime).

20. Sync Your Resume (CV) Style

Simple Strategy

We like to think of ourselves as individuals. Yet there comes a time when we have to conform to a certain extent to get in the door. Conforming your resume (CV) falls into this category. Don't apply a "one-size-fits-all" approach to writing your resume (CV). Ironically, your resume (CV) isn't really about how you see yourself. Instead, it's about how your future employer should see you in their organization. Every industry has different standards, formats and styles when it comes to crafting a resume (CV). Some industries like punchy one-pagers. Others prefer a lengthier multi-page minutiae-based document. You must know which path is best for your intended industry. Not knowing the specific particularities of an industry is a worrisome sign to your potential employer that you don't care or know enough about their industry. So, although it may seem like common sense, just by applying common sense to common practice will give you a competitive edge by syncing your resume (CV) style to your target industry. Speak to insiders, ask recruiters and review sample styles online to get a feel for the industry.

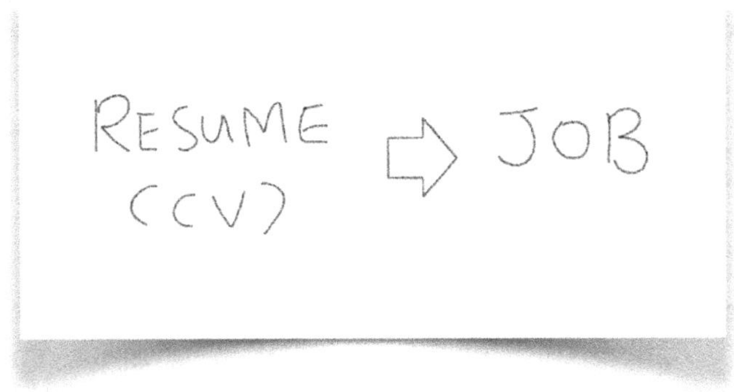

Simple Example

Business Resume (CV): Single page (with succinct summaries and bullet points)

Academic Resume (CV): Multi-page (with publication list and academic awards)

21. Get Inside Information (Legally)

Simple Strategy

In economics, the Efficient Market Theory holds that every market actor has all available information needed to make perfectly optimal decisions. Theory is great for classrooms. But theory often breaks down in the real world. One reason is that not everyone has exactly the same information. Does a billionaire hedge fund manager have the same market information as a taxi cab driver? To some this seems ludicrous and incredulous. There's a saying in finance, "Don't trade unless you have an edge." To gain a tactical edge in your job negotiations, you need information. This is because information is power in your job negotiations. You don't need complete or perfect information. You just need (relatively) *more* information compared to the other Job Candidates competing for your same position. Often this involves getting information from insiders. This doesn't mean getting confidential, non-public insider information. This means getting insights, strategies and perspectives from those who have or are doing what you want to do career-wise. You could peruse public information available online, such as corporate or industry websites, newsletters, blogs and socials. But you should augment this by meeting directly with people who are or have worked for the same firm or industry as what you're aspiring towards. Emulate those who you want to become (and ignore those who you don't want to become). Try connecting via LinkedIn or other socials. If you don't hear back after a week or so, try sending a short email. Give a quick strategic summary about yourself (based on what the recipient may find useful or interesting, not just your perspective). Offer to buy lunch or coffee. And make it succinct — professionals are busy. Which is why, if you don't hear back, don't fret. It's a numbers game.

Simple Example

LinkedIn Message: Hi Tessa! I'm a business major at University Zeta. I was so impressed with your past deals with Firm Alpha, which happens to be exactly where I'd like to work after graduation next year. I know you must be super busy. But would it at all be possible for me to buy you coffee and chat briefly about career advice? It'd be so amazing to get your thoughts. I really don't know many people in the industry, which is why I'm reaching out to you via LinkedIn. By the way, I noticed you played volleyball during college — I happen to be a starter for my university's volleyball team — what a small world! Thanks so much, Mannie

22. Audit Your Social Media

Simple Strategy

Privacy is a relic of the past. Know that anything you post on your socials — TikTok, Instagram (IG), Facebook/Meta, X (Twitter), LinkedIn, Reddit posts, articles and blogs — is close to public knowledge and access. Your future employers have an incentive to investigate who they'll be hiring. After all, employers don't want the risk of negative blowback based on something you did, even if it was before an offer was made to you. So do an audit of all your social media posts — from your potential employer's perspective, not yours. If you wouldn't want all your coworkers to see any of your posts, then you may want to scrub it. If you can't do it all by yourself, there's an app for that! Even if you signed the offer, you're not completely safe. There's likely provisions within your employment contract that gives the employer the right to fire employees based on certain trigger events. So, blogger (and social media users) beware!

Simple Example

Don't Do This:

Twitter (X) Post by Candidate: Hey all, I just interviewed at Firm Z. Can't believe how stiff and corporate they are! Made me wonder if they were human — or corporate cardboard cutouts. Reminded me of a scene straight outta *The Matrix*. But hey, if they pay me enough I'll do and be whatever. Update: they just made me an offer — and I accepted — can't wait to be part of the corporate cardboard cutout crew lol!!

23. Act Like You Have The Job Already

Simple Strategy

Most people think about job negotiations as a situation of how to get a job. Flip the script. Treat the interview like you already have the job. So, your task during the job interview is to make this impression felt. This mental mind shift will lead to greater confidence and better performance. From the Recruiter's perspective, it'll show you're confident, and confidence is usually predicated on prior successes. From your Job Candidate perspective, it helps you mentally step into the shoes of the job. But to pull this off, you must actually know what you're talking about. To know what you're talking about, you must have done your research. As part of your research, tell yourself, "As an Analyst at Company Z, what would be my tasks today and how exactly would I get them done?" or "What would be my typical day for the job?"

Simple Example

Tell and ask yourself: *As* an associate at Firm X, what would be my *typical day*?

Tell and ask yourself: *When* I'm given a job offer, what terminology would I expect to use for doing the job?

Think to yourself: I'm qualified for the job. So, my next step is to demonstrate my qualifications and experience during the interview. Both sides will be better off by getting to yes.

24. Forming First Impressions

Simple Strategy

Like it or not, based on a seminal study at Princeton University, your Interviewer will have an initial impression of you in less than a second of seeing you. This may not seem fair. But who said life was ever fair? Knowing this, create a script in advance for what you'll say, and how you'll say it. Pay particular attention to the first few seconds of the interview. Think of it as sketching out your first few plays in a sports game. By doing this, you'll be better positioned for success from the very first second of the game — known as your job interview.

Simple Example

Script for the First Few Seconds of an Interview

Interviewer: Glad to meet you. Please have a seat.

You: Thank you for taking the time to meet me! I've heard so many wonderful things about your Firm. And based on all my research, I'm highly impressed by the work you've done in terms of environmental causes.

25. Value Your Value

Simple Strategy

Price and *value* are different. *Price* is what you *pay* for something. *Value* is what you *get* from something. In job negotiations, price is your salary. Your value is a function of your specific skills and experience that you bring to the table for an organization to reach its stated mission. In your job negotiation, remember this: your price should reflect your value. So first calculate your value to your target organization. This can be in both monetary and non-monetary terms. Only after you calculate your value — then and only then — come up with your price (total hiring package) that reflects your value. Remember: you don't get what you deserve, you get what you *negotiate.*

Simple Example

Candidate A's Value:

* Coding Skills: $125,000/year
* Negotiation Skills: $35,000/year
* Leadership Skills: $25,000/year
* Your Total Value (Your Worth) = $185,000
* Salary (Price) = $185,000

26. Find Your Unfair Advantage

Simple Strategy

Not all people are built the same. Arguably every one of us are better at doing at least one thing better than others. This is what's known as an *Unfair Advantage*. An Unfair Advantage gives you an advantage over others who are in or aspiring towards the same job or industry as you. Unfair Advantages exist everywhere. Know your Unfair Advantage. Is it your gift of gab and forming human connections? Eloquent writing? Crunching numbers? Thinking visually? Being multicultural or multilingual? Write down all your strengths and see which of these strengths are your Unfair Advantages. Then leverage your Unfair Advantages to your career advantage.

Simple Example

Unfair Advantage in Business: a business with an exclusive product, preferential government treatment or monopoly has an Unfair Advantage over its competitors

Unfair Advantage in Athletics: an athlete may have an Unfair Advantage in basketball by being taller, faster and having access to physical training facilities and trainers

Unfair Advantage in Entrepreneurship: a startup founder may have an Unfair Advantage if he or she comes from a well-connected family or school with many potential mentors and investors

Your Unfair Advantages:
1. (List Your Unfair Advantage #1)
2. (List Your Unfair Advantage #2)
3. (List Your Unfair Advantage #3)

27. Know Thyself (Self-SWOT Analysis)

Simple Strategy

Socrates once proclaimed, "To know thyself is the beginning of wisdom." If you don't know yourself, what are the chances your future employer will know you? No one, including your employer, will hire someone they feel they don't really know. This is called human capital risk. This is why it's important to know yourself and your inner constitution. What are your values? What's your "Why" (purpose)? What are you willing to stand up for? What do you want out of a particular job and why? You may not have permanent answers. But the important task here is to ask these questions, write down your current answers and constantly update them as you encounter new people, situations and experiences. Even more specifically, perform a Self-SWOT analysis. SWOT is a powerful tool taught in MBA programs (Strengths, Weaknesses, Opportunities, Threats).

Simple Example

Strengths (S): Highly social. Enjoy complex problems. Love to learn.

Weaknesses (W): Get bored quickly. Tend to go quickly but broadly. Passionate interest in many areas can lead to lack of long-term focus.

Opportunities (O): Engage with people for lifelong learning. Read books on diverse subjects. Write down takeaways from projects, books and experiences.

Threats (T): May be perceived as uninterested in long-term projects. May not form many deep relationships among certain people. Analysis may be broad and big picture.

- Your Self-SWOT

Strengths (S): (Write 1-3 Strengths)
Weaknesses (W): (Write 1-3 Weaknesses)
Opportunities (O): (Write 1-3 Opportunities)
Threats (T): (Write 1-3 Threats)

28. Do A Ted Talk Thought Experiment

Simple Strategy

Do you know exactly what you want to do for the rest of your life? If you don't yet, don't fret. Not knowing is more common than uncommon. We are all works in progress. Getting to an answer often takes tinkering with different jobs and sectors. As Auguste Rodin heralded, "Nothing is a waste of time if you use the experience wisely." But there's another simple way to find your career calling. And it can be done in the comfort of your home (and mind). It comes in the form of the following TED Talk thought experiment.

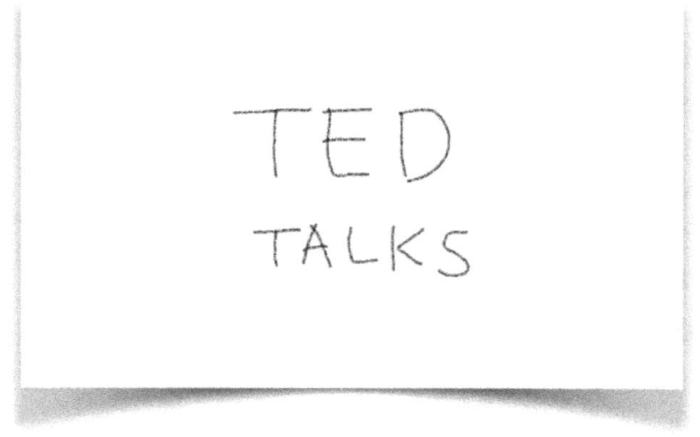

Simple Example

TED Talk Thought Experiment

Imagine: that you're waiting behind a theater curtain. You're standing there as the keynote speaker for a sold out TED Talk. You hear the announcer telling your audience of all your prominent accolades and accomplishments, followed by, "And so, without further ado, please give our next TED Talk keynote speaker a warm welcome!" You then confidently walk onto the stage.

Thought Experiment: What accolades and accomplishments would you ideally want in your hypothetical TED Talk introduction? What specific TED Talk topic do you see yourself giving? And finally, what specific types of people would you want listening to your keynote presentation (entrepreneurs, politicians, hedge fund managers, academics, activists or something other group)? Once you answer these fundamental questions, you know one possible end destination to your career journey. This then empowers you to reverse-engineer your end destination to where you are today. What series of steps, big or small, do you need to take to get you to your final stop? If you don't know where you're going, you'll go nowhere. But if you know exactly where you're going, you'll rocket yourself to your chosen career path.

29. Evaluate Your 3E's (Ethics, Emotions And Economics)

Simple Strategy

A self-reflective dashboard diagnostic gives you important feedback for your career trajectory and final destination. One useful dashboard diagnostic is the 3E Framework (Ethics, Emotions and Economics). The 3E Framework determines the importance to you of each of the 3E's — Ethics, Emotions and Economics. The key to completing the 3E Framework is to input specific *estimated percentages* for each of the 3E's, within a job context. Specifically, how important are ethics, emotions and economics to you? *Ethics* can represent things like what *doing the right thing* means to you, and what makes up your moral compass. *Emotions* can represent the importance of how you *feel* about aspects of the job. How important is it to feel fulfilled, happy or appreciated at your job? *Economics* is often the most straightforward of the 3E's, which denotes how important *money* is to you when it comes to work. Is money the end-all, be-all? Is a job just a series of profit-driven economic transactions or should it be something else? Every person is different. So, it shouldn't be surprising that each person may have different values in their 3E Framework.

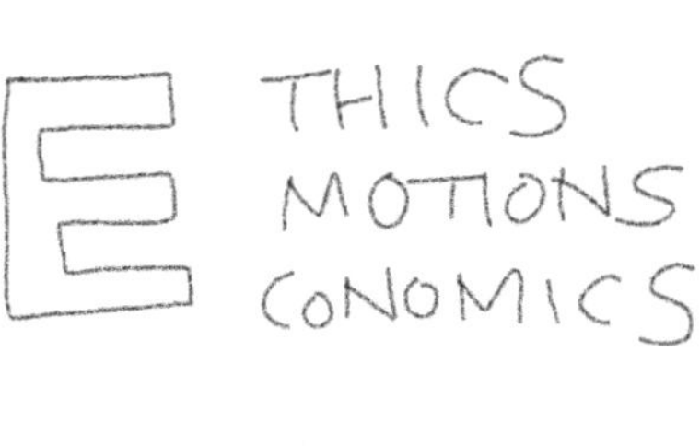

Simple Example

Banker

Ethics: 10%
Emotion: 5%
Economics: 85%

International Aid Worker

Ethics: 80%
Emotion: 10%
Economics: 10%

Your 3E's

Ethics: x%
Emotion: x%
Economics: x%

30. Know Your Tribe

Simple Strategy

It's important to know what type of people and environment you enjoy. Do you vibe in a more casual or formal work setting? Do you work better at the office or from home? Do you like bosses who are down to earth or strictly business? If it helps, think of the ideal work environment and the people in it. Sketch it out. Then ask, "What job or industry best fits this sketch?" Doing this will help you know your tribe.

Simple Example

I like creative environments filled with fun and creative types.
I feel like working with other creative types can be exciting and
exhilarating. At the same time, being able to spend time on my
own terms helps me draw out my creative ideas most
effectively. My ideal manager would be self-effacing yet
extremely competent. I'd love to be in a work environment
where people are free to laugh and express themselves, rather
than feel like a cog in a corporate machine.

31. Know Your Vibe

Simple Strategy

Finding your *flow state* is key to a happy and fulfilled career trajectory. The concept of *flow* is a state of complete absorption and energized focus where time seems to fly with unlimited possibilities, while reaching your maximum flow state. Flow arises from a balance between challenge and skill. When the challenge of an activity is too high, some experience anxiety and struggle to maintain focus. But when the challenge is too low, boredom and disengagement set in. Flow occurs when the challenge is just right, pushing individuals to their limits, while still allowing them to feel a sense of competence and control.

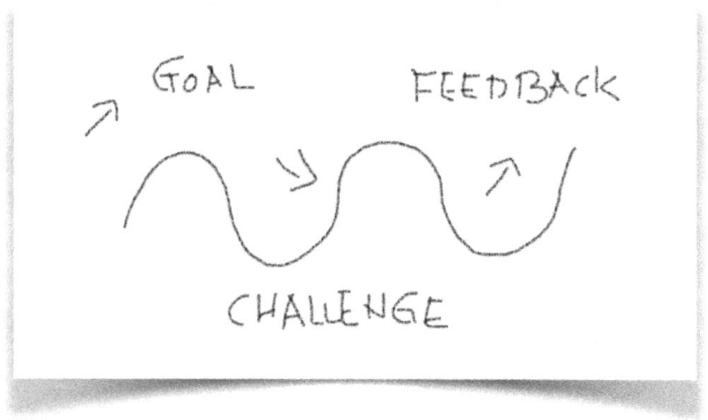

Simple Example

To cultivate flow in our daily lives:

1. Set Clear Goals: define specific and achievable goals for your activities, providing a clear direction and purpose.

Goal: I'll read and summarize four books per month to further my career.

2. Increase Challenges: gradually increase the difficulty of tasks to keep them stimulating and prevent boredom or disengagement.

Goal: I'll achieve three increasingly difficult tasks this month.

3. Seek Feedback: actively seek feedback on your performance from other people.

Goal: I'll seek feedback from three friends and three family members for each book summary.

4. Minimize Distractions: create an environment free from distractions that can disrupt your focus and concentration.

Goal: I'll go to a quiet place to read books and strategize on my career.

5. Practice Mindfulness: engage in activities that promote mindfulness and present-moment awareness, such as meditation or yoga.

Goal: I'll spend the first ten minutes of every morning focusing on mediation or yoga.

32. Pursue Your 3P's (Purpose, Passion, Profit)

Simple Strategy

What's one framework to navigate your career arc? Think of 3P's: Purpose, Passion and Profit. To find your *Purpose*, ask yourself, "What am I good at doing?" Think about your strengths in any area, without using any career labels, such as title or position. It could be social, academic, linguistic or anything else. To find your *Passion*, look at your actions rather than your words. What do you read, write or think about during the week? Look at your open browser tabs, bookmarks and things you've clicked on online as bread crumbs. Themes in books, podcasts, blogs or movies can also reflect your particular passion. Finally ask yourself, "What combination of my Purpose and Passion overlap to translate into *Profit*?"

Simple Example

Purpose: Reading, writing and analyzing
Passion: Persuading other people
Profit: Becoming a lawyer

33. Feedback Is Fabulous

Simple Strategy

If people don't know enough about you, they won't be able to hire you. This is why firms spend millions on advertising. But it starts with you. So spread a positive and catchy narrative about yourself. Share your resume (CV) to as many people as people. Studies suggest that it's not your direct circle of contacts that lead to a career opportunity, but your second level of contacts who are more likely to help you get a job. You can also apply guerrilla marketing techniques for your job search. Even if the application instructions tell you to apply to one specific source (HR or website link), do research on who the likely team members would be if you were hired. Then send your resume (CV) and a very short self-introduction via e-mail and/or LinkedIn direct message to them (especially the most senior person whom you share something in common). Working professionals are extremely busy. So, send your email or message on a Wednesday or Thursday (Mondays and Tuesdays have super-packed schedules, and on Fridays, people tend to start leaving or begin mentally checking out before the weekend). If you're applying to a more traditional company or sector, use both first and last name. If it's a more casual company or sector, you may be able to use just the person's first name. The more hands and eyeballs on your resume (CV), the higher your chance for success.

Simple Example

Dear Bridgette,

Hope you're doing well. I'm a 2nd-year MBA student and would love the opportunity to work for your team at Nonprofit A.

I've already applied to a position through the on-campus recruitment team. But I would really appreciate any feedback or suggestions you could provide in terms of whether my background would be a good fit.

Thanks so much!

Best regards,
Jan

34. Be A Bullet Point Bargainer

Simple Strategy

If you want to be remembered, keep things punchy. To keep things punchy, think and talk in bullet points. When preparing for your job interview, write a Top 3 list of bullet points that pertain to possible interview questions. Then rank order your bullet points them from most to least relevant and likely.

Simple Example

Recruiter: So, why don't you tell me about yourself?

You: There are three things you need to know about my qualifications for this position.

* First, I have over five years of direct experience at my previous firm working on exactly the same issues as your team.

* Second, I have a solid academic foundation for the job having earned top grades in some of my university's most difficult courses and subject matter, in which my same work ethic and knowledge used at school can be leveraged to help your team.

* Third, I love to learn ways to improve myself. By doing this, I can continue to contribute as much as I can each and every day to your team and the Firm.

Each and collectively, these factors, among many others, make me the ideal Job Candidate for the position.

35. Don't Use ChatGPT As CheatGPT

Simple Strategy

When it comes to writing your cover letter, some would say to never use ChatGPT (or similar technologies). Some counterargue by saying that ChatGPT should be the go-to for writing cover letters since it saves time and does a decent (albeit non-final version) job of writing cover letters. The best equilibrium approach is to utilize the best of both words using "A vs. B" (A/B) testing where two versions are put head-to-head to determine which document version would have the higher likelihood of getting you to the next (interview) stage. Think of it like a one-on-one face-off in sports, except that it's document versions instead of athletes competing (A/B) for your final winning approval. For Version A, write out your own cover letter without ChatGPT. For Version B, have ChatGPT write out your cover letter (with some minor customization on your part). Then show both A and B cover letter versions to a group of three people (ideally from different backgrounds and perspectives). This is your G-3 Summit. The majority opinion — for Cover Letter Version A or B — should generally be the version to submit for a particular career opportunity. Or alternatively, you can blend the two versions into a single cover letter version.

Simple Example

Step 1.

Version A: Your cover letter written by yourself

Version B: Your cover letter written by ChatGPT (or similar technology)

Step 2.

Give Version A and Version B cover letters to your G-3 (Group of Three)

Step 3.

Use the cover letter version that the G-3 majority believes will be most successful

36. Know Your Audience

Simple Strategy

In daily life, we instinctively become different versions of ourselves depending on our audience. If you're a college student, how you speak to your dorm roommates would be very different than how you speak with your professors. If you're working in politics, how you speak to your colleagues would be different than how you speak with big-ticket donors. How we conduct ourselves, including how we speak and address questions, is specific to our audience. So, knowing your audience is paramount. Similarly, for job interviews, know your audience. Will your potential hiring committee members be more formal or casual? What values or objectives would they support and seek in Job Candidates? What specific industry terms or buzzwords would they find competent-sounding and persuasive? Thinking about your audience and viewing yourself through their lens is the difference between being good and being great for your next interview.

Simple Example

Interviewer: Why do you want to work for our company?

You: I've been following your company for a while now, and I'm really impressed with its commitment to innovation and sustainability. I'm particularly interested in working on [list your specific project or initiative]. I believe that my skills and experience in [list your relevant skills] would be a valuable asset to your team, and I'm confident that I could make a significant contribution to your company's success.

37. Mindfully Meditate With Mozart

Simple Strategy

Studies show that listening to classical music can increase your cognitive performance. Psychologist Frances Rauscher and her colleagues at the University of California, Irvine, coined this the "Mozart Effect." The study found that college students who listened to a 10-minute excerpt of Mozart's "Sonata for Two Pianos in D Major" performed significantly better on a spatial reasoning task compared to those who listened to silence or pop music. This may have to do with the classical composition's complex structure and dynamic musical patterns that help to stimulate the brain. You may not be a superfan of classical music or Mozart, but you're probably a superfan of trying as many things as possible for the best outcome in your job negotiation. So put on those earbuds and start moving to Mozart (but if you just can't stand classical music, other musical genres with complex rhythms may also have positive effects).

Simple Example

* **Listening to Mozart:** to boost your cognitive performance

* **Listening to nature sounds:** to improve your focus, concentration and memory

* **Listening to white noise:** to improve focus and concentration (by blocking out distracting noises)

* **Listening to music you personally enjoy:** to reduce stress, increase dopamine levels and enhance your memory

* **Listening to podcasts with people who come from the same background or industry as those in your job interview:** to mirror the language and ambience of your interview

38. Be Nice Or Be Nixed

Simple Strategy

Treating everyone nicely has many advantages during a job interview. It makes a good impression, which in turn, increases your chance of getting the job. Being nice, in which you're friendly and engaging with the people you meet, also helps to build rapport. Building rapport helps make both you and the Job Interviewer more comfortable within an otherwise formal and potentially awkward situation. Always being nice also helps you to get information or tips, such as from the receptionist, other employees and even other Job Candidates waiting for their interview. Even one piece of actionable advice can tip the scales in your favor. Treating everyone nicely can also help elevate your own emotional state. If you feel good about yourself, it'll manifest during the job interview. Good vibes translate into good outcomes.

Simple Example

* Be polite and respectful to everyone you meet, from the administrative assistant to the Interviewer

* Smile and make eye contact

* Be a good listener

* Ask thoughtful questions

* Thank everyone for their time (given their busy schedules)

39. Envision A Typical Day

Simple Strategy

To get what you want in your next job negotiation, you must know what you want — in a very exact and specific sense. Imagine you're working at your dream job right now. Write your typical 24-hour day, from the time you wake up, until the time you go to sleep. For example, my book *24 Hours with 24 Lawyers: Profiles of Traditional and Non-Traditional Lawyers* has exactly this future-focused mission in mind. Apart from forcing you to think about your dream job in a very specific way, visualizing a typical 24-hour day also gives a sneak preview of your aspirational career. Ask yourself, "Is this the type of career and life that I *really* want?" The answer should be an emphatic "yes!" An instant and emphatic yes is a true yes. On the other hand, if you have to think it over too much, or if you tell yourself, "Well, I guess I could do it if they pay me enough," then these are red flags. Remember: think before doing. Stay patient. It's better to know now than later that your dream job may not be so dreamy after all.

Next, create a vision board of your dream job. Close your eyes to envision the city, the office building, the floor layout, your exact working area along with the look and feel of the entire workplace. Is everyone sitting in an open office? Is it a quiet or noisy working space? Is the vibe calm and laid back or full of hustle and bustle? Look online or in magazines for visuals that match your vision and put it all into one place. Seeing is believing.

Simple Example

Digital Nomad Entrepreneur - Vision Board

* **7:00 am:** Wake up in a bungalow to the sounds of waves crashing along the beach.

* **7:30 am:** Do yoga, practice intentional meditation and positive affirmations under the warm sun and gentle ocean breeze.

* **8:00 am:** Drink an espresso and eat granola along with fruit yogurt while mindfully eating.

* **9:00 am:** Begin your work day with a zoom brainstorm session with other amazing digital normal entrepreneurs.

40. Know Bargaining Styles

Simple Strategy

Everyone negotiates differently. How a person negotiates is known as a *bargaining style*. Richard Shell of The Wharton School of Finance has a useful bargaining style self-assessment. It distills your answers to 30 short questions to one of five bargaining styles: *Competitor, Collaborator, Compromiser, Avoider* and *Accommodator*. Step one is to estimate your dominant bargaining style using Shell's self-assessment survey. Knowing your dominant bargaining style will help you understand yourself better with questions like: "Why am I using a particular bargaining style during my job negotiations?" "Does this bargaining style get me good results?" and "Would other bargaining styles help me get my worth?" Step two is, before your interview, estimate the possible bargaining styles of your Job Interviewers (if known) using information you gather from publicly available sources, other people who've been interviewed at the same organization or word of mouth. Once you're actually in the interview room, continue to ask yourself, "Okay, so what is this particular Job Interviewer's bargaining style?" Like any self-assessment, the framework is a snapshot in time based on your thoughts and feelings at the time of the self-assessment. In other words, it's a selfie rather than a livestream of your bargaining styles. Admittedly, like any self-assessment, it may not be perfect. But few things in life are perfect in practice. As the adage goes, "It's better to be generally right than exactly wrong." Pair this knowledge with information about your Job Interviewers from public sources (organization's website, LinkedIn and news outlets) to get a fuller picture of the people you're aiming to persuade.

Simple Example

Potential Bargaining Styles

* **Competitor Style:** enjoys the bargaining process, but may bulldoze over others leading to ruined relationships

* **Collaborator Style:** views the bargaining process as a problem-solving expedition, which may be unnecessary for simple job negotiations

* **Compromiser Style:** seeks to close out bargaining sessions by "splitting the difference" based on fairness, transparency and/or efficacy, but may leave options on the table

* **Avoider Style:** tends to dislike and avoid bargaining situations, and often prefers delaying a negotiation to gather more information or seek to conduct the interview in an online setting (rather than in-person)

* **Accommodator Style:** places a strong emphasis on relationships, but if such tendency to be driven by relationships is known in the marketplace, the relationship can be "held hostage" by counterparties to get better negotiation-related terms and conditions

41. Walking Out Is A Strategy

Simple Strategy

In a job interview, you may find yourself in a David versus Goliath situation, in which you're playing David (the Underdog) and the Interviewer is playing Goliath (the Big Dog). Know that you hold complete self-autonomy over how you view and carry yourself during the interview. Expectations matter. If you think you'll be bulldozed over, your implicit and/or explicit tells and actions may lead to a self-fulfilling prophecy. To help boost your autonomy, tell yourself you have the power to say no. If the offer by the Interviewer is below your breaking point (your Reservation Point), then you should seriously consider walking out as a strategy. Before walking out, confirm the offer terms (to ensure you haven't misheard or misunderstand it). Then if you still believe it's below your breaking point — and assuming it's a firm and final offer — clearly communicate why you're walking out in the most professional manner possible. Don't feel guilty or bad about walking out. Why would you say yes to a deal that doesn't get your worth? Even if you say no, you've gathered information, such as what salary and conditions the Firm is willing to offer, which will be potentially very useful for future negotiations with the same or different organization in the same industry or area. The possibility also exists that the Firm may contact you again on the working assumption that if you're willing to advocate so strongly on your own behalf, then you'll likely advocate just as assertively on behalf of the Firm's interests. In any negotiation, you want the counterparty to believe that it's strategically more beneficial to have you on their side as an invaluable team member — than on the other side of the table — as a high-performing and highly competent competitor.

Simple Example

Interviewer: Based on your background, skills and experience, I'm prepared to offer you a starting salary of $55,000 per year. Would you be willing to accept this offer?

You: I truly appreciate the time and consideration put forth by you and the Firm in making the offer. After careful consideration, I regret to say that I'm unable to accept the offer at this time. If, however, the offer can be revised to make it more competitive with market rates, I would be happy to consider it. Thank you again and I look forward to keeping the communication lines open.

42. Be A Ninja Negotiator (Using Psychology And Jedi Mind Games)

Simple Strategy

Most people only focus on what they physically see as a source of influence during interviews. As another tool in your toolbox, focus your mind on the invisible influencers that incorporate psychology and Jedi mind tricks. Robert Cialdini is one such academic expert who incorporates such elements into his actionable research (known as social psychological influences). As Cialdini's seminal studies suggest, the best type of negotiation is one using persuasion and influence, such as *reciprocity, scarcity, social proof* and *authority.*

Simple Example

* **Reciprocity:** complimenting the Recruiter on something she or he has accomplished, such as "I'm really impressed by your success track record for your clients."

* **Scarcity:** emphasizing a skill or experience that very few other Candidates possess, such as "It was an honor to place first in a moot court competition against the best law schools in the country."

* **Social proof:** noting that your skills are highly sought after based on several other job offers already received, such as "Among the three job offers I've received, this one appears very promising."

* **Authority:** conveying that you're an expert in a particular area based on a well-cited article you've published, such as "If you're interested in my further thoughts on the topic we discussed, I'm more than happy to refer you to my recent article in the *Harvard Business Review*."

43. Think Fast And Slow

Simple Strategy

Nobel Prize winner, and social psychologist Daniel Kahneman, argued that our brains have two distinct types of thinking systems, Type 1 (*Thinking Fast Mode: emotional brain*) and Type 2 (*Thinking Slow Mode: rational brain*). Type 1 thinking links to "fight or flight" instinctual impulses. Type 2 thinking links to "rational" decision-making and analysis. In theory, we should all be Type 2 thinkers and decision-makers. But in practice, studies suggest that when Type 1 and Type 2 systems collide and go head-to-head (often during a highly complex decision), Type 1 (emotional brain) is often the victor in the epic battle for your brain. So, during your job interview, make a best guess regarding the estimated type of thinking mode of your Interviewer. Will your Interviewer be more Type 1 (Thinking Fast Mode: emotion-driven) or Type 2 (Thinking Slow Mode: logic-driven)? If you believe the Interviewer is more of a Type 1 thinker, use words like "I *feel.*" If you believe the Interviewer is more of a Type 2 thinker, use words like "I *think.*"

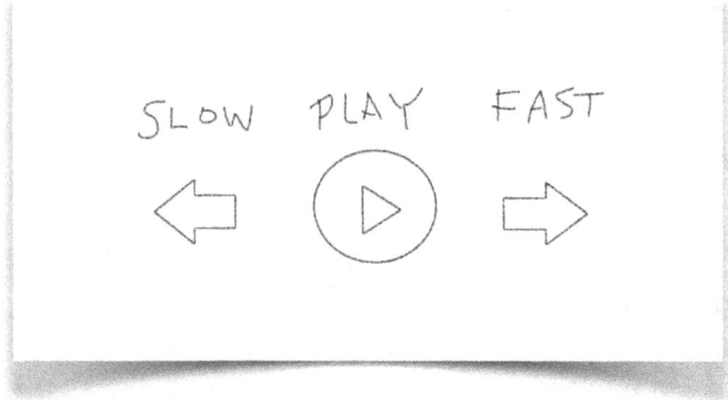

Simple Example

Scenario 1

Interviewer (Type 1 Thinker: emotion-driven): My *gut* tells me that the best person for this job is someone who's a natural born leader. Which begs the question: do you feel like you have the inherent qualities to be a leader in our organization?

You: Yes, I definitely *feel* that I'm absolutely a natural born leader.

Scenario 2

Interviewer (Type 2 Thinker: logic-driven): Based on my data and research, I think that those who come from an engineering background tend to succeed at our Firm. What are your thoughts?

You: Yes, I certainly *think* I have a high likelihood of succeeding at your Firm based on my highly quantitative engineering background, which aligns perfectly with the position and its many task-oriented duties.

44. Say "I Don't" (Not "I Can't")

Simple Strategy

Can one word serve as a directional switch in your next job interview? According to several studies, there's a notable impact of using the words "I *can't*" versus "I *don't*" when answering interview questions. One study found that using the phrase "I can't" can lead people to believe they have less control in a situation. In contrast, using the phrase "I don't" can lead to a belief that more control exists over a situation. Research suggests this is because "I can't" is associated with a sense of helplessness and failure, while "I don't" is associated with agency (freedom) and choice. Another study suggests that using "I don't" can be helpful for breaking bad habits, resisting temptation and making difficult decisions, while another study found that using "I don't" can be helpful for setting boundaries, saying no to requests and avoiding making excuses. So, if you want to express and empower yourself, say "I don't" rather than "I can't."

Simple Example

Addressing a lack of experience

Don't say: I can't handle this task because I lack the requisite experience,

Say this instead: *I don't* have direct experience in this particular task, but I have a strong foundation in related areas and I'm a quick learner. I'm confident in my ability to learn the necessary skills to excel in this role

Don't say: I can't answer that question because I've never been good at numbers,

Say this instead: I don't have an immediate answer to that question, but I'm confident in my ability to research and provide a thoughtful response given some time. Can I have the opportunity to give you a thoughtful answer by the end of the business day or another timeframe that works for you?

45. Show You're In The Top 20%

Simple Strategy

Did you know that the top 20% of people in organized structures yield 80% of total output? This "80/20 rule" is known as the Pareto Principle. It can be applied to a wide range of situations, from business and finance to personal productivity and self-improvement. In the context of business, the 80/20 rule suggests that 20% of your customers will generate 80% of your revenue. This means that it's important to focus your efforts on serving your most valuable 20% of customers who represent 80% of revenue. Similarly, 20% of your products will likely generate 80% of your profits, so it's also important to identify and prioritize your most important products. The 80/20 rule is a powerful tool that can help you focus your time and energy on the activities that matter most. So, your job negotiation strategy is to show that you're in the top 20% in as many ways as possible — to demonstrate you can provide 80% of total value compared to other Job Candidates.

Simple Example

Focus on the top 20% of job-related deal points:
instead of trying to negotiate every single aspect of the job
offer equally, focus on the 20% of issues that will derive 80% of
value for you. Separate from salary, this could include job
scope, environment, promotion potential, benefits, vacation
time, bonuses and/or the flexibility to work remotely.

Showcase your top 20% achievements: identify which
parts of your professional and/or academic experience and
outcomes are in the top 20%. For sales numbers, utilize a
commonly-used metric to indicate that your overall P&L
(profit and loss) are objectively and statistically in the top 20%.
For academics, show that you were on the Dean's List,
graduated in the top 20% (*summa cum laude, magna cum
laude* or *cum laude*) or part of the Student Body Council (to
signal leadership traits). These are all indicia of evidence that
you're in the top quintile, and thus, capable of creating 80% of
an organization's overall worth.

46. Be A Scout (With A Growth Mindset)

Simple Strategy

In a job negotiation, two classic characters arise onto the scene: the Soldier and the Scout. The *Soldier* sees the negotiation playing field as a battlefield, in which the Soldier's duty is to vigorously and aggressively defend a certain territory. In the Soldier's viewpoint, might makes right, more is better and relationships don't matter much. In contrast, the *Scout* sees the negotiation playing field as an information acquisition game, in which the Scout's duty is to gain a tactical advantage by securing an information advantage. The Scout sees information as power and influence. The Scout acts like an intelligence officer using a combination of hard skills (number crunching, data analysis) and soft skills (emotional IQ, effective communication). From a sociological perspective, the Scout would have a *Growth Mindset*, who views challenges as opportunities for learning, while not being afraid to fail. Within the Growth Mindset, failure is feedback for future improvements. People with a Growth Mindset believe that intelligence and talents are teachable and learnable, as opposed to those with a *Fixed Mindset* who believe that they're static and unchangeable. Which one should you choose? Based on years of sociological research, being a Scout with a Growth Mindset are the golden keys to sustainable success in both work and life.

Simple Example

Steps to a Growth Mindset:

* **Believe in yourself and your ability to learn and grow.** Say, "I used to pay college tuition to learn, but now in my current role, *I'm* the one getting paid to learn."

* **Embrace challenges and setbacks as opportunities for learning.** Ask yourself, "What are my takeaway lessons from this moment (for future improvement)?"

* **Focus on effort and improvement, not just on outcomes.** Ask yourself, "How can I improve by 1% in the future?"

* **Celebrate your successes, no matter how small.** Say, "I feel such gratitude that I live and work in this amazing time and place!"

* **Seek out feedback and mentorship from others.** Ask,
  "In what ways can I improve to reach and exceed the
  targeted key performance metrics?"

Part 2: During The Job Interview

47. Give A Range (Of Possible Salaries)

Simple Strategy

One of the most pivotal moments of your job negotiation will be when the Recruiter asks the question, "So what's your salary expectation?" Most fear this question. But don't *react* (instinctively/emotionally). Instead, *respond* (strategically/rationally). Do research by not asking "What exact salary do I want?" but rather "What *range* of possible salaries would I find acceptable, as part of a total compensation package?" While salary is one thing, it's not everything. Focus on the big picture. Another way of reverse-engineering your range of possible salaries is to first target your ideal (reasonable) starting salary (your ideal point, known as your Aspiration Point), and then create reasonable ranges of salaries that pivot around it. By offering a range of salaries, rather than a specific salary point, you've enabled a wider playing field for negotiation. A wider playing field is better for both sides. And from the Firm or Recruiter's perspective, your showed skills in widening the playing field will also make you appear more reasonable, smart and savvy.

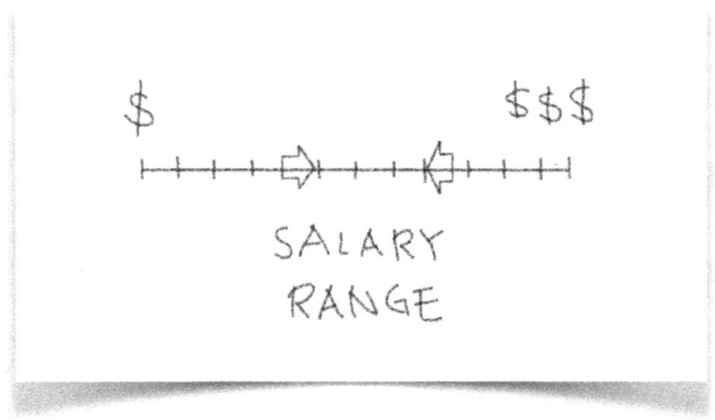

Simple Example

Recruiter: I think now may be a good time to ask for your salary expectations relating to the position?

You: I'm glad you asked this very important question, so that we both know that we're aligned on this issue. What would be the general *range* or budget for the position?

Recruiter: We generally hire for this position within a certain salary range, but before disclosing it, I'd first like to get your salary expectations.

You: I appreciate you sharing that information with me. That's very helpful. Based on the research I've done, I believe a starting salary range between $80,000 and $100,000 could be perfectly reasonable for the duties and responsibilities tasked for the position. Admittedly, this is a somewhat wide range, and so the more I get to know about the people, the role and the organization itself, the more I'd be able to provide further specificity regarding my salary expectations.

48. How To Answer The Unanswerable

Simple Strategy

You've heard the adage, "expect the unexpected." This holds true for job negotiations. The unexpected are known-unknowns — things you know you don't know. But you can only control what's controllable. Fortunately known-unknowns are more controllable. An example of a known-unknown is being asked a question and you not knowing the right answer. What to do in this case? So glad you asked! A smart reply to a question where you don't know the answer is to provide a *framework* (methodology) towards *getting* to the answer. In other words, if you can't provide the answer, provide a way to *get* to the answer. Although this may not give the exact answer, this type of response signals that you have the ability to adapt to new situations and provide a useful analytical approach to cut through the clutter. It helps to distinguish the signal from the noise. This type of job interview strategy is particularly useful for positions and sectors that deal in complexity and uncertainty, such as technology, finance and management consulting. The key to answering this question effectively is to demonstrate your ability to think critically, ask the right questions, gather relevant data as well as make informed estimates based on imperfect and ever-changing situations.

Simple Example

Managing Director: To get a sense of your thinking processes, how would you answer the following hypothetical question: what's the likelihood that a former professional athlete is currently working for our Firm?

You: While it's difficult to predict with absolute certainty the likelihood of a former professional athlete working for the Firm, what I can provide is an informed estimate based on working models, assumptions, certain data and my current understanding of the industry. So, to get started with the analysis: assuming that approximately 10% of professional athletes transition into corporate careers — while factoring in our Firm's highly visible reputation and focus on sports, teamwork and leadership — we may be particularly attractive to former athletes seeking to utilize their skills in a business setting above the 10% baseline figure. Therefore, I estimate that there is a 15-20% chance that a former professional athlete is currently working for the Firm.

49. Don't Use "But"

Simple Strategy

When the Job Interviewer says something and you disagree, try to find something about the Interviewer's statement that you find agreeable, even if you don't agree with everything said. Seek commonalities, not differences. Then use the words "at the same time" rather than "but" before giving your counterpoint or example (unless you want to emphasize the words that you found disagreeable following "but"). The reason? Many people tend to focus on the words that follow the word "but," while ignoring the part preceding it ("I really like the job description, but…."). Some common similarities could include being an alumni of the same school, having lived or traveled to the same city or area, supporting the same sports team or sharing the same hobbies. Similarities bond people ("You love matcha lattes, that's amazing, so do I!"). Which is one step closer to getting to yes.

Simple Example

Say: I appreciate your salary offer, *at the same time*, I would be very curious if it at least equals what others have been given at your organization for the same roles and responsibilities.

Don't Say: I appreciate your salary offer, *but* it doesn't come close to my salary expectations.

50. The Hot Coffee Advantage

Simple Strategy

Job Candidates are viewed on many factors, including competence and warmth. Recruiters and your future colleagues want people who not only get the job done, but who are also decent and nice human beings. It may seem obvious, but after you're hired, you'll not only be spending a lot of time with your coworkers — they'll also be spending a lot of time with you! So, Interviewers are generally looking for someone who gets the job done while getting along with others. One secret way of boosting your likability quotient involves something quite often overlooked: holding a hot drink (such as a hot coffee). If we were perfectly rational judges, the type of drink someone's holding shouldn't have any bearing on how much we like that person. But scientific studies show otherwise. Research indicates that people holding hot (or warm) drinks were seen as, well, warmer and kinder. This, in turn, made hot drink holders seem more approachable, friendly and trustworthy. Why would this be? Humans subconsciously associate warmth with social connection and belonging. Holding a warm beverage subconsciously signals an invitation for interaction, making the individual appear more approachable and inviting (referred to as Social Thermoregulation). Warm beverages also evoke feelings of coziness and relaxation, subconsciously triggering positive emotional responses in observers. This can lead to a perception of friendliness and trustworthiness (known as Emotional Cues). Warm beverages can also promote the release of oxytocin, a hormone associated with bonding, trust and social connection. So even if you're an iced coffee type of person, if you want to be viewed as more warm, trustworthy and likable — skip the ice cubes — and instead opt for the steamy hot beverage.

Simple Example

Coffee Shop Barista (en route to your interview): Would you like your drink hot or iced?

You: Hot please — steaming hot!

51. Master The Mirroring Strategy

Simple Strategy

Mirroring is a technique used in negotiations to build rapport with your counterparty. Mirroring involves *subtly* repeating the other person's words, phrases or body language. Mirroring is effective since you're using select words, gestures and social cues of the Interviewer, which can help create a sense of connection and trust. This in turn increases your chance of reaching a mutually beneficial agreement. The Mirroring Strategy can be used for both verbal and non-verbal communication during your interviews.

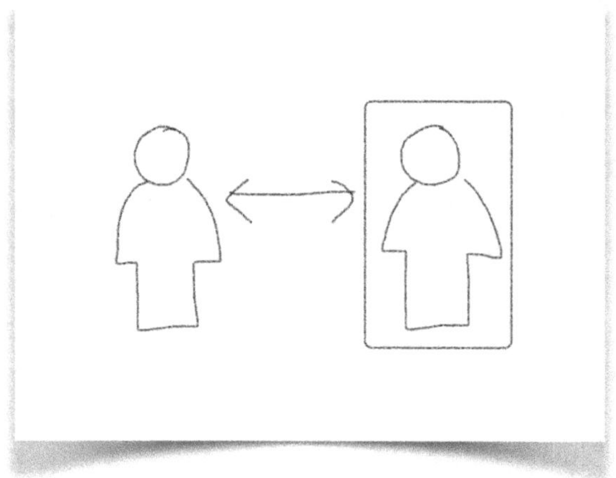

Simple Example

* **Repeating keywords:** when the other person mentions a specific salary, benefit or other negotiation point, repeat back certain keywords to them. This shows that you're listening carefully and that you understand their priorities.

* **Matching body language:** if the other person is leaning forward and making eye contact, do the same (with some subtlety). This shows that you're engaged in the conversation and that you're interested in what the other person has to say.

* **Using similar language:** if the Interviewer is using formal language, mirror parts of the formal language and word choice being used (but don't completely copy it, because this would be weird). If the Interviewer is using more informal language, you can relax your own tone and make your word choice more informal. This helps to create a sense of rapport and connection — an invisible influence that gets the Interviewer to feel more comfortable with you.

52. Be Interested, Not Interesting

Simple Strategy

A job interview is essentially a social interaction between you and the Firm and its representatives. You may think the goal during the interview should be to talk about yourself and why you're qualified for the job. But avoid this temptation. Instead, practice the mantra of "be interested, not interesting." This means you should pivot towards listening to the needs and wants of the Interviewers, rather than always trying to put the spotlight on yourself. Embodying this engagement strategy can have significant positive ripple effects. By demonstrating genuine interest in the organization, the role and people involved, you as the Job Candidate, can establish yourself as thoughtful and engaged. The "being interested, but not interesting" approach will also tend to foster trust, rapport and a more collaborative (integrative) negotiation process. It's not about feigning interest or adopting a superficial persona. It's about cultivating genuine curiosity about your future coworkers, actively listening to their thoughts and showing appreciation for their perspectives.

Simple Example

Recruiter: It seems you have a wealth of experience. Can you tell us more about you and why you want to work for our organization?

You: Well, I know your firm is focused on corporate social sustainability (CSR) initiatives, which is exactly my focus area. Based on this, I think my experience will be quite helpful in furthering your organization's amazing efforts in the CSR space. Having said this, I'm excited to hear where you see your organization going, including its CSR efforts and initiatives for the next few years?

53. Say "No" To Saying "No"

Simple Strategy

Sometimes you need to say "no" in a job negotiation. After all, it's very clear and direct. If clarity is your main objective, a "no" reply leaves little to the imagination. At the same time, a blunt "no" can have negative repercussions. Admittedly, putting your foot down and saying "no" occasionally may be what's needed. But when saying "no" becomes your main response mechanism, it can be potentially detrimental to your job negotiation for several reasons. For one, saying "no" can put the other party on the defensive, making them feel like their ideas are being rejected or not fully heard. This lost in translation moment can lead to a communication breakdown and deterioration in trust. Saying "no" can also restrict the flow of creative thinking and prevent the exploration of potential solutions. Even more, it can give a sense of inflexibility and unwillingness to compromise, potentially hindering the process of finding common ground and reaching a compromise. Know that the word "no" isn't the only word in the dictionary to denote the sense that you don't agree. Instead of "no," based on the situation, use alternate approaches to convey a similar meaning.

Simple Example

You're negotiating a salary with your potential employer. They offer you $70,000, but you were hoping for $80,000.

You: I appreciate your offer of $70,000. I've conducted thorough research on salaries for similar positions for the industry and location, and the average seems closer to $80,000. However, I'm willing to discuss creative options if we can also consider certain benefits such as flexible work arrangements or additional vacation time.

54. Never Say "Yes" (Say "Yes, if...")

Simple Strategy

During your job negotiation, certain questions may require a direct "yes" answer. Instead of saying yes, strategically say "yes, if." Then link the "yes, if" to one or more other items you want included in your overall job package. Saying "yes, if" instead of simply "yes" can be a powerful strategy for achieving your desired outcome (known as Linkage Strategy). By framing your response with "yes, if," you're also acknowledging the other party's position and signaling your willingness to come to a consensus. While doing so, you're also somewhat surreptitiously introducing your additional conditions or considerations. This approach not only helps you get your worth, it also gives the impression that you're a team player who considers the views of your potential future coworkers, not just your own.

Simple Example

Recruiter: I'm happy to offer you a starting salary of $70,000. Can I assume you're willing to accept this offer?

You: *Yes, if* we also include a reasonable performance bonus structure and a work-from-home option — which I believe may lead to an overall compensation package I could accept.

55. Smiling Is A Strategy

Simple Strategy

Smiling can be a powerful tool in your job negotiations. It can help build rapport with the Interviewer, make a positive impression and convey confidence. One research study showed that participants who smiled during their job interviews were rated as more likable, approachable and trustworthy, while also more likely to receive a job offer. Another study showed that those who smiled were rated as having higher leadership potential — even when their qualifications and experience were similar to other participants who didn't smile. Studies also suggest that smiling increases your cognitive function (thinking) by 31%. At the same time, it's important to use smiling strategically. For example, it's important to give a genuine smile. A fake smile won't have the same effect as a genuine smile. Make sure you're smiling because you're happy and confident, not because you're trying to manipulate the situation. It's also important to smile at the right times, such as when you first greet your Interviewer, while introducing yourself as well as when answering questions. The avoidance of smiling can also have negative effects, making you seem nervous, insincere or socially awkward. You should also smile, but not too long, usually for around two to five seconds. Smiling seems awkward only if you make it awkward. So, practice smiling — it makes you smarter and more likable — what's not to smile about that?

Simple Example

* **When asking for a higher salary:** *Smile* as you make your request. This will help you to convey confidence and positivity.

* **If the Interviewer raises objections to a certain request or point of view:** *Smile* as you respond. This will help you stay calm and collected, while making what you say appear more reasonable.

* **Smile as you chat with the Interviewer before the negotiation begins (if the opportunity presents itself):** *Smiling* will help you build rapport and make a positive impression, which will have positive spillover effects once your job negotiation begins.

56. Don't Give The First Offer (As A Job Candidate)

Simple Strategy

One common question in job negotiations is whether to give the first offer — or wait for your boss or Interviewer to give their first offer. Generally speaking, giving a *credible* first offer sets an "anchoring effect," in which future deal points revolve around the first offer. So generally, it's better to preemptively give the first offer to set an anchor in a negotiation. *But* there's an important exception. As a Job Candidate, you don't have as much information about the role compared to the Firm (this imbalance is referred to as "asymmetric information"). If you don't have the requisite information to make the first offer, it's better to wait for the first offer from the Firm. In a *Harvard Business Review* article, the authors advocated for the "wait for the first offer" approach. One reason is that the Job Candidate can then use the information gained from the counterparty's first offer to make an effective counteroffer, which would more likely be accepted. The HBR article also noted that waiting for the employer's first offer can make the Job Candidate appear more confident and valuable. Since negotiation power is a function of information, waiting for the first offer — rather than being tempted to make the first offer — will give you important inside information to wage an effective counteroffer. This in turn will increase the chance of receiving a more favorable job offer to get your worth.

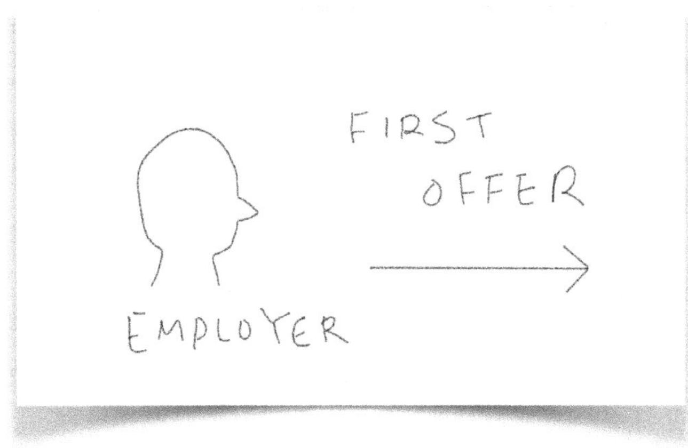

Simple Example

Recruiter: What would be your expected starting salary?

You: That's an excellent question, and one I'm glad we're able to discuss together. Since you probably have more details on the role and allocated budget for it, I'd be interested in your thoughts on what starting salary would reflect today's competitive market rate?

57. Ask For The Budget (Allocated For The Position)

Simple Strategy

Most Recruiters are given a set budget (upper and lower bounds) of what can be offered to Job Candidates. If you have this information, it'll be a strategic advantage. Don't be timid about asking. If you don't ask, you don't get. So just ask. What's the worst that can happen? If asked professionally, posing questions to the Interviewer will generally not be viewed as unprofessional or awkward. Most sophisticated professionals will understand that asking is a signature feature of a multi-layered job negotiation process. If anything, asking this type of question signals that you're a savvy negotiator who's serious about the role and organization. Several studies support the notion that asking about a potential employer's budgetary information achieved better outcomes, including higher salaries and greater satisfaction with the job negotiation process. One study observed that budget disclosure led to greater trust, more accurate expectation setting and a more cooperative negotiation process.

Simple Example

Interviewer: I'd be interested in hearing your exact salary expectations for the job.

You: To make a more informed decision, I'd be curious to know what the budget is for this position?

Interviewer: The budget for the position is $150,000.

You: That sounds reasonable to me. I believe that figure makes a good starting point towards moving to a final overall remuneration package composed of both monetary and non-monetary benefits.

58. Show You're Willing To Learn

Simple Strategy

One person can't know everything. Knowing that no one knows everything can be comforting and even empowering. As a case in point, if you don't know the answer to a particular question in a job interview situation, just say you don't know — but then quickly express your genuine willingness to learn more about the area. Expressing a willingness to learn has several distinct advantages for both you and organization. For you, it signals that you have a Growth Mindset (discussed earlier in this book), who's more open to new ideas and adaptable to change. It also emphasizes potential over perfection, while also demonstrating that you're eager to be part of a learning-oriented culture. Expressing your willingness to learn further signals that you have a proactive approach to professional development, which aligns with what most professional organizations want. It also shows your current or potential employer that you're committed to staying relevant and contributing value over the long-term. This makes the case that an investment in you will be beneficial, not just now, but also down the road. This approach also indicates that you're open to feedback, coaching and development, signaling that you're adaptable and can take on different roles or responsibilities within the organization.

Simple Example

Interviewer: Since you're applying for a financial planning position, can you explain to me the relationship between the Federal Reserve benchmark rate and bond prices?

You: That's a very interesting question. At this point, I'm not exactly sure of the perfect answer, but I would certainly look forward to learning more about this area once I join your team. As you can see from all my accomplishments in my resume (CV), I'm a quick study and a consummate learner.

59. Use Percentiles (As Evidence Of Excellence)

Simple Strategy

Most people think of a resume (CV) and cover letter in terms of words only. At the same time, because organizations are increasingly reliant on numbers and data (think: spreadsheets and statistical analysis), words shouldn't be the only persuasive proof of your professional competency. So, sprinkle your resume (CV) and cover letter with numbers (total sales volume, revenue, profit and so on). And importantly, use percentages as part of your story. Research demonstrates that applications using percentages were rated more favorably than those that used words only, suggesting that percentages in your resume (CV) can increase your chance of getting hired by employers. Percentages are also a powerful way to quantify and highlight your accomplishments, while demonstrating your skills and achievements. Percentiles allow you to go beyond vague verbal statements (such as "excellent" or "significant") to provide concrete evidence of your impact compared to your coworkers or peers. Numbers also help you highlight your "value add" to a project and provide a specific way to distinguish yourself from other Candidates. Using numbers and percentages also help signal career progression to support the notion that you're a "top x%" worker who meets or exceeds organizational and industry benchmarks.

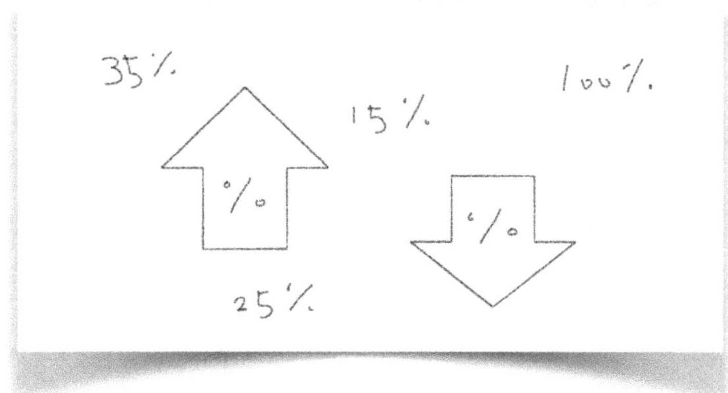

Simple Example

* Grew website traffic by 35% through targeted social media campaigns, leading to a 38% increase in online sales.

* Managed a team of 10 engineers to deliver three projects on time and within budget, resulting in 12% cost savings and 15% added revenue.

* Increased sales by 25% in the first year, exceeding key performance targets by 23%.

60. Be Evidence-Based (Not Esoteric)

Simple Strategy

Providing evidence of excellence during job negotiations is crucial to demonstrating your value to potential employers and landing a dream job offer. Research reflects that using evidence-based communication strategies were associated with higher salaries, better benefits packages and more senior job titles. Negotiators who used specific pieces of evidence to support their achievements were further perceived as more credible, persuasive and prepared. Even with such studies, many Job Candidates often default to generic words to describe their experience and expertise. Be different. Provide specific evidence to support your claims in your resume (CV) and cover letter. Be specific with specific achievements, specific transactions and specific figures. This will help separate you from the pack. Highlight specific projects and contributions, including your specific role, responsibilities as well as measurable outputs. Demonstrate how your work directly impacted the company's bottom line, growth or success story. In an interview setting, discuss your accomplishments in detail, including describing the context, challenges, tasks and specific actions you took that led to specific successful results.

Simple Example

Interviewer: Your resume (CV) mentions you improved logistics efficiency at your previous company. Can you elaborate on that?

You: Certainly. At Alpha Dog, Inc., we were experiencing delays and rising costs in our product delivery process. This was impacting customer satisfaction and putting a strain on our budget.

(Specific Evidence) I identified that a major bottleneck was in the packaging and labeling stage. The manual process was time-consuming and prone to errors, causing delays in shipment. I proposed and implemented a semi-automated system that streamlined the process significantly.

(Impactful Results) This new system not only reduced packaging time per unit, but it also minimized labeling errors, leading to fewer product returns and happier customers.

Furthermore, the reduced labor costs associated with the automation helped us achieve 12% savings annually.

(Process Improvement) The success of this project highlights my ability to identify inefficiencies, develop solutions and implement them effectively. I'm a strong believer in optimizing processes to ensure smooth operations and cost savings.

61. Use Helpful Hand Gestures

Simple Strategy

Hand gestures are a powerful tool to enhance your nonverbal messaging — adding another powerful tool to your job negotiation toolbox. It's crucial however to use hand gestures appropriately and strategically to avoid appearing unnatural or distracting. Specific helpful hand gestures include using open palms, such as showing your palms or using a spread-hand gesture. Doing this conveys openness, honesty and a willingness to listen. Using open palms also expresses enthusiasm or receptiveness to feedback. Another helpful hand gesture strategy is the use of steepled hands, where you put your fingertips together (to form the shape of a steeple). Doing this projects confidence, composure and thoughtfulness. Try not to overuse steepled hands though since this runs the risk of being perceived as aloof, contrived or arrogant. You can also try illustrative gestures, such as using hand movements to mimic actions or concepts you're discussing with your Interviewer. Using illustrative gestures can help bring your words to life and make your communication more engaging. At the same time, beware of cultural norms. If you're not quite sure what hand gestures to use, benchmark the person interviewing you. If the Interviewer uses open palms, for example, you can do the same. Overall, if done strategically and correctly, using hand gestures as part of your overall nonverbal communication toolkit can help you make a more positive and lasting impression on potential and current employers.

Simple Example

You (*using a steepled hand gesture*): I'm confident my skills and experience align perfectly with the requirements of this position. I'm particularly excited about the opportunity to contribute to the company's growth strategy and help it achieve its fiscal goals.

62. Being Imperfect Makes You Perfectly Likable

Simple Strategy

Many people believe that the goal of a job interview is perfection, and based on this, aim for a perfect performance. At first instance, perfection may seem like your goal. But consider this: when was the last time you met a "perfect" person? In the real world, there isn't a perfect person or perfect thing. So, when Interviewers in the real world encounter a person who seems perfect, it can have the opposite intended effect. Ironically, making mistakes may actually *help* you in job negotiations. Specifically, the *pratfall effect* — also known as the clumsiness effect — is a psychological phenomenon where individuals are perceived as more likable and competent after making a *minor* mistake or revealing a humanizing flaw. This effect can be particularly advantageous in job negotiations, where Job Candidates may inadvertently make a small error or occasionally stumble over words. The reason? Small flaws, within otherwise highly competent Candidates, show a sign of authenticity, while humanizing an individual's persona. It also helps create a more memorable impression from the Interviewer's perspective, especially after a long day of interviews with similarly-qualified Job Candidates.

Simple Example

You: I'm so excited about the opportunity to discuss this position with you. However, I must admit, I haven't had a chance to update my address on my resume (CV). I just moved a few days ago. I apologize for this and will provide an updated version of my resume (CV) shortly.

Interviewer: No worries, that happens to the best of us. I'm sure you can still provide me with a good overview of your experience and accomplishments so far.

63. Reframe Your Job Interview (As A Career Conversation)

Simple Strategy

The word "interview" can conjure up images of a one-way interrogation where an innocent victim is being stress-tested for answers in front of a powerful panel of decision-makers. But instead play a reverse mind game to optimize for success. Instead of framing things as a "job interview," reframe it as a two-way "career conversation." Studies suggest that a two-way conversation — characterized by active listening, empathy and mutual understanding — can lead to greater trust and rapport. It also results in more favorable outcomes for both parties. Think of the interview room as a proxy coffee shop (or other comfortable place) where you're speaking to a potential mentor about his or her view of a particular position. Reframing the interview into a career conversation will make you more relaxed, which in turn, will boost your confidence. Interviewers will sense your boosted confidence, increasing the chance that you and your qualifications will be viewed more positively. It's also worth knowing that Interviewers are ordinary people just like you and me. Underneath their lofty job title, they also have their particular preferences, hobbies, family duties and life dreams. With this in mind, treat your career conversation as an exciting opportunity. So, listen and pay attention, and feel free to ask questions like you would in any normal conversation. Remember, for the career conversation to get to a yes, both sides need to agree together in a collaborative effort. In this sense, you're "interviewing" the Interviewers as much as they're interviewing you.

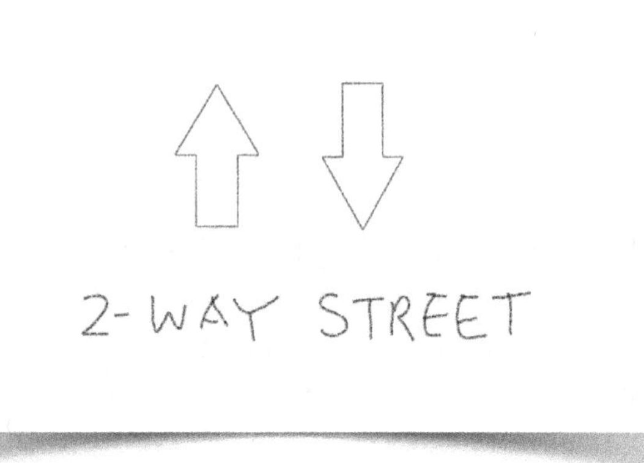

Simple Example

Interviewer: To get a sense of you as a person, we on the hiring committee would be interested in knowing about the most recent book that you've read.

You: As an avid reader, I'm so glad you asked. I'm actually reading two books right now. One book is *Crying at H Mart*, which is an amazing story of a daughter's relationship with her deceased mother based on the shared foods they ate together. To me, it highlighted the importance of human connections and empathy, which I think are especially relevant to this job. Another book I'm reading is *Persuasion: The Hidden Forces That Influence Negotiations*. It's filled with amazing strategies on how to persuade and nudge people!

Interviewer: I see you have a very inquisitive mind with wide interests. I've actually heard great things about both books. Would you recommend them?

You: Definitely! The two books balance and complement each other perfectly. I'd also be curious as to the books you've read recently that had a positive impact on your current position.

64. Show The Write Stuff

Simple Strategy

Demonstrating your writing ability during a job interview is crucial for showcasing your communication skills and suitability for roles that require strong written expression. You can use several strategies to highlight your writing skills. One way is to provide writing samples in areas most relevant to the job and industry you're targeting. Published works in notable journals, websites or other sources will be viewed as highly impressive, even if writing isn't the main task for the job. Other examples of written work can be more informal if the writing is still high quality, such as in blogs and other online outlets. Other formal or informal written pieces could be useful, such as written reports, op-eds, articles in trade journals or other online forums. You should also quantify the impact of your writing or writing-related projects. Provide concrete examples of how your writing made a positive impact, such as increasing website traffic, generating leads or influencing decision-making. This demonstrates the added value you bring as a writer. You can also think about adding an appendix section to your resume (CV) that lists all your relevant writings with the article title, date of publications along with their weblinks (if online).

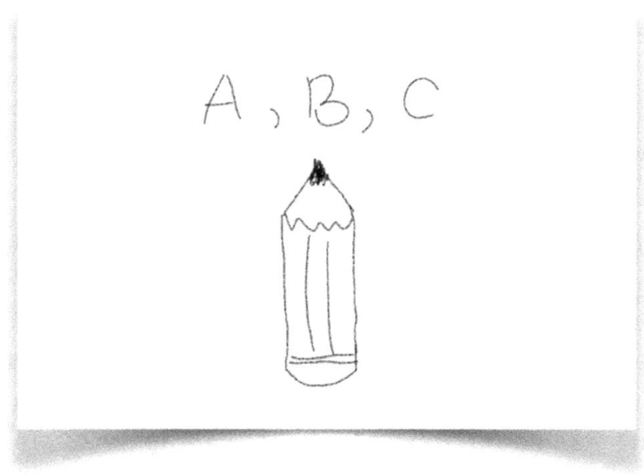

Simple Example

Interviewer: I see you have a portfolio of writing samples. Can you tell me a bit about them?

You: I'd be happy to do so. I've included a variety of samples that showcase my writing skills in different contexts. For example, this blog post I wrote for Marketing Company A resulted in a 20% increase in website traffic. This white paper I authored for a Technology Firm B was cited in several industry trade publications. And this sample press release I drafted for Nonprofit Organization C helped boost media coverage by 33% for a very worthy animal advocacy event.

65. The Subtle Art Of Eye Contact

Simple Strategy

One of the oldest pieces of advice for a job negotiation is to make eye contact. Research suggests that eye contact increases perceptions of trustworthiness and dominance, which can lead to more favorable negotiation outcomes. This then begs the question, "In what way should I make eye contact?" Aim for eye contact about 60-70% of the time. This demonstrates your engagement and attentiveness without being overly intense. Use eye contact strategically, for instance, when emphasizing key points, expressing enthusiasm for a certain opportunity or signaling your confidence in certain areas. When doing this, try to distribute your eye contact equally among those who are in the interview. Also, avoid focusing your eye contact on just one or a subset of the interviewing panel. Eye contact should complement both your nonverbal as well as verbal communication. At the same time, avoid staring or fidgeting, which can convey social awkwardness or nervousness, and be conscious of cultural, corporate and industry norms.

Simple Example

Important Moments to Make Eye Contact:

* Initial introduction
* Responding to Interviewer inquiries
* Emphasizing key points
* Signaling enthusiasm
* Responding to offers and counteroffers
* Concluding the job interview

66. Beware Of Biases

Simple Strategy

In a perfect world, everyone would be perfect. Unfortunately, an ideal world may clash with real world facts and circumstances in the form of various biases. One type of bias is Implicit Bias — also known as Unconscious Bias — which can manifest in various forms during job negotiations, often subtly and unintentionally. One type of implicit bias is gender bias, in which a Hiring Manager might inaccurately assume, for instance, that a female Candidate is less assertive or demanding than a male Candidate (leading to a lower initial offer or less flexibility in a job negotiation). Another example is race, cultural and ethnic biases. Here, an Interviewer might make assumptions about a Job Candidate's skills or qualifications based on race, culture or ethnicity, potentially undervaluing the Candidate's abilities or contributions. One of the more prevalent biases is Confirmation Bias. This can occur when a person focuses on information that confirms a Recruiter's pre-existing biases about a Candidate — while overlooking or downplaying evidence that contradicts those biases — thus confirming a preexisting belief, prejudice or stereotype.

Simple Example

Gender Bias: A female Candidate might be praised for her "soft skills" such as her teamwork and communication skills, while a male Candidate is praised for his "hard skills" such as his technical expertise and problem-solving acumen.

Race, Culture or Ethnic Bias: A Job Candidate from an underrepresented group might be assumed to be less qualified than a white Job Candidate, even if the underrepresented Job Candidate has the same or better experience and qualifications.

Confirmation Bias: A Recruiter with a negative impression of a Job Candidate might be more likely to interpret the Job Candidate's behavior negatively, even if such behavior is neutral or ambiguous.

67. Notice Naughty Nonverbals

Simple Strategy

Nonverbal communication plays a crucial role in job negotiations, since it can impact the perception of your competence, confidence and professionalism. Positive nonverbal cues, such as relaxed shoulders and uncrossed arms, can reinforce your strengths and enhance your negotiation efforts. Negative nonverbals, on the other hand, can undermine your credibility and lower your chances of landing a dream job. To maximize your chance for success, convey positive nonverbals and display open nonverbal postures so you're viewed more positively. But beware of possible unconscious or habitual closed postures or gestures — such as looking at your digital device — as well as crossing your arms or leaning away from the Interviewer. These types of nonverbals can convey defensiveness or lack of interest. Negative facial expressions, such as frowning, scowling or generally looking unhappy can also convey negativity or lack of interest, even if you your intent is trying to look serious. There's often a fine line between appearing serious and appearing unhappy. To see where your facial features fall in the spectrum, take a selfie while striking your "serious" pose — and judge for yourself how you may be perceived by others in a job recruitment setting.

Simple Example

Interviewer: So, how do you see your skills and experience contributing to our team?

You (*while crossing your arms and leaning slightly away from the Interviewer*): I think I can bring a lot to the table. I'm a hard worker and I'm willing to go through the painful process of long hours to get the job done if the pay is competitive enough.

68. Use Positive Words (So You Appear More Positive)

Simple Strategy

Using positive words during your job negotiation can influence others to view you more positively. Studies have shown that people who use positive language are seen as more likable, competent and trustworthy — compared to those who use negative language to describe other people and situations. This is because positive language conveys a number of positive qualities, such as enthusiasm, optimism and confidence. Using positive language can also make you appear more persuasive. When people feel positive, they're more likely to be open to new ideas and information. This means that using positive language can help get your point across. At the same time, it's important to use positive language in a genuine and authentic way. If you're not sincere about the positive language you're using, most Interviewers will see right through it. In contrast, when you use positive language thoughtfully and with sincerity, you'll make a powerful impression on others, and in turn, influence others to view you more positively.

YOU'RE
AWESOME!

Simple Example

Avoid saying: I'm not sure if I'm completely qualified for this high-demand job.

Say this instead: I'm super excited about the opportunity to leverage my entire set of skills and experience to contribute to this position and your amazing team!

69. Splitting The Difference (Is Splitting Your Worth)

Simple Strategy

If you were a hostage negotiator, would you be willing to split the difference, if what was considered being split was an actual human life? Even the thought of splitting a person should sound absolutely abhorrent (unless it's part of a magic trick). But if splitting a person seems repulsive, why are people so often willing to split the difference for anything that's of importance or high value? Yet this happens literally everyday in negotiations. When it comes to job negotiations specifically, splitting the difference can potentially equate to splitting your total worth. Knowing this, would you now be so easily willing to split the difference? Employers are hoping you say yes to this easy way out (for them). This is because employers often have much stronger bargaining power over you, since employers typically have multiple Job Candidates to choose from. So, by agreeing to split the difference, you (as a Job Candidate) may be grossly undervaluing your skills and experience — stopping you from getting your worth. The end result could be potentially splitting the difference (halving) your total salary and benefits package. Rather than relying on splitting the difference, it's better to approach job negotiations with a focus on understanding the employer's needs and priorities. At the same time, identify your own strengths and value proposition, and assertively advocate for them during your job negotiation. This will increase your chances of landing your dream job offer that aligns with your career goals and aspirations — and getting your worth.

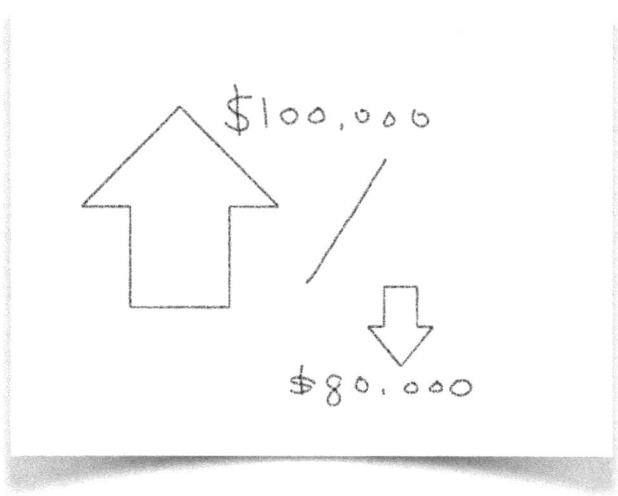

Simple Example

You: I believe $100,000 would be a reasonable starting salary.

Employer: Well, after conferring with my team, we've concluded that our normal starting salary for this position would be $80,000. But how about this, let's split the difference at $90,000?

* Possible impact of splitting the difference:

- If you accept the employer's offer of $90,000, you'll be "splitting the difference" between what the employer wants ($80,000) and what you want ($100,000), which stops you from getting your worth.

- By "splitting the difference" with your salary, you may feel undervalued and later leave the organization earlier than if you held your ground.

- "Splitting the difference" could also lead to regret and extreme job dissatisfaction during your tenure at your job, which could lead to a self-fulfilling prophecy for failure.

70. The Magic Word (To Get Your Target Salary)

Simple Strategy

Would you ever take a road trip without any idea of where you're going? Probably not. Yet so many people don't think concretely about where they're going on their career roadmap. So, what should you do? Flip the script. First, pinpoint your final destination. Then work backwards to your starting point. What's the best way to do this? Good news, it involves a secret word: "assume." According to recent research, using the word "assume" conveys confidence in your value and worth to an organization when used in the following way.

Simple Example

Interviewer: We're impressed with your qualifications and experience. Our initial salary offer for this position is $80,000.

You: Thank you for the offer. I've thoroughly researched the market rate for this position's level of experience and responsibility, and I'm confident my value in terms of salary is $100,000 or more. *Assume* I accept a job offer with a $100,000 starting salary, what would it look like in terms of the overall package, including monetary and non-monetary benefits?

71. How To Strategically Stall (When Asked A Quixotic Question)

Simple Strategy

One nightmare scenario for many people is freezing in front of a job interview panel when asked a challenging question. What you don't want to do is seem like a deer staring in the headlights. So, what's the best way to give yourself a few precious moments to think of a thoughtful response during a high-stakes job interview? There are several approaches. You could acknowledge the question and then ask for clarification. This may be helpful as a strategic stalling technique, even if you're already fairly clear on the context. Another method is to use transitional phrases like, "Hmm, that's a very good question. Let me think about that for a second." Yet another transitional phrase you could use is "I think we could unpack that into several parts." This shows that you're taking the time to craft a thoughtful response — rather than blurting out a rapid-fire, uncensored and unedited thought stream. You could also relate your reply to a previous professional or personal experience that illustrates your skills, experience or qualifications. This can make your response more engaging and memorable while giving you more time to think. At the same time, avoid using excessive fillers or rambling responses, since this may make you appear unprofessional or unprepared. One final strategy is to answer the question with a question or series of questions.

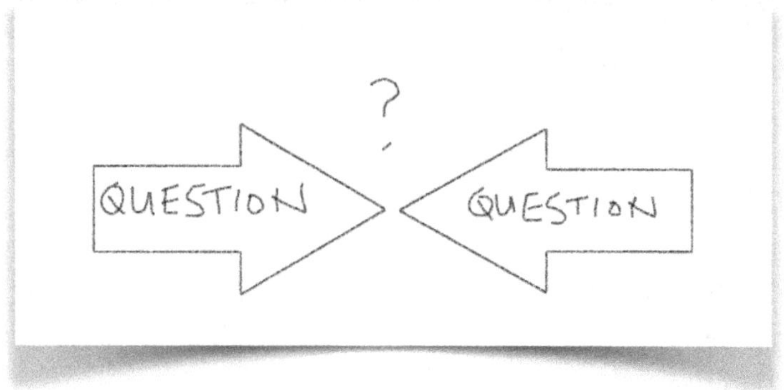

Simple Example

Interviewer: If you had to guess how many basketballs would fill the room we're sitting in right now, what would be your specific methodology?

You: That's a very interesting question. To unpack the question, do you mind me asking some questions of my own, to get to a possible answer?

Interviewer: Of course.

You: Thank you. First, what would be the diameters of the basketball? Is it an NBA regulation basketball for adults, or a smaller version for children? Is it fully or partially inflated? What are the dimensions of this room?

72. Avoid (Excessive) Apologies

Simple Strategy

Saying "sorry" from time to time in a job negotiation may be common practice, but if done excessively, it can have several unintended cascading effects. This is because apologizing too frequently can convey a lack of confidence in your abilities and worth. It may also signal to the employer that you're unsure of your value, and thus, potentially willing to accept less than your true worth. Apologizing can also inadvertently give away power and put you at a disadvantage during a job negotiation. It suggests that you're willing to take the blame or responsibility for relatively minor perceived shortcomings, even if not directly your fault, which could weaken your negotiating position. Constant apologies can also raise doubts about your competence and suitability for the role. It may lead the employer to question your ability to handle the responsibilities of the job or represent the company effectively. Either case would erode your value, potentially leading to a lower salary or fewer benefits.

Simple Example

What to do in lieu of apologizing excessively

Acknowledge and address concerns: if you made a mistake or have something to rectify, acknowledge the issue directly and address it promptly and succinctly. Take responsibility and propose solutions without resorting to outright apologies.

Maintain confidence: project confidence in your abilities and the value you bring to the table. Speak assertively, make eye contact and use positive language to convey your competence and worth.

Focus on solutions: instead of apologizing for issues beyond your control, focus on what you *can* control, namely in proposing solutions and demonstrating your problem-solving skills. Show how you can overcome challenges and contribute positively to the company or organization.

168

Use different wording: instead of saying "I'm sorry" or "I apologize," use third person language to create a cognitive distance between yourself and the situation at hand, such as "The outcome of that last project was regrettable and not exactly ideal…but this led to some invaluable reflection on how to improve the process going forward."

73. Concise Is Nice

Simple Strategy

The ideal number of words to use in a job interview depends on the specific industry, context of the question and the Candidate's ability to convey his or her thoughts clearly and concisely. It's important to strike a balance between being too brief and being overly verbose. Being too brief can make you, as the Job Candidate, appear unprepared, uninterested or lacking in substance. On the other hand, being overly verbose can make you appear unfocused, disorganized or unable to convey your point. Giving long-winded, meandering responses may also bore your Interviewer or make it more difficult for the Interviewer to follow your train of thought. Certain research shows that Job Candidates who used more words were viewed as slightly more articulate and confident, but less likable and less trustworthy. The takeaway: use as many words as necessary to make your point, but no more.

Simple Example

Range of words to use

For short-answer questions: aim for concise responses that directly address the question and provide the most relevant information.

For open-ended questions: provide more detailed responses that showcase your knowledge, experience and thought process that get to an answer. However, avoid going on tangents or providing unnecessary details.

For storytelling questions: use vivid language and descriptive anecdotes to illustrate your points. However, keep your stories concise and relevant to the question.

When elaborating on your strengths: provide specific examples of your accomplishments and contributions to demonstrate your value. Quality over quantity is key. Complement descriptive words with numbers or rankings.

74. How To Give Smart Summaries

Simple Strategy

When asked to provide a summary about a piece of written work — such as a book, article or blog — there's an effective way to provide smart summaries. In short, it's all about structure. Within the structure, you have freedom to deviate. The structure is to first provide the specific argument of the written work. You can use the words, "author's point" or similar language. If you want to get fancy, use the word "thesis," which has a similar meaning but more formal feel. After conveying the written work's point, break it down in terms of a bullet point list in terms of evidence or arguments that support the written work's point or thesis.

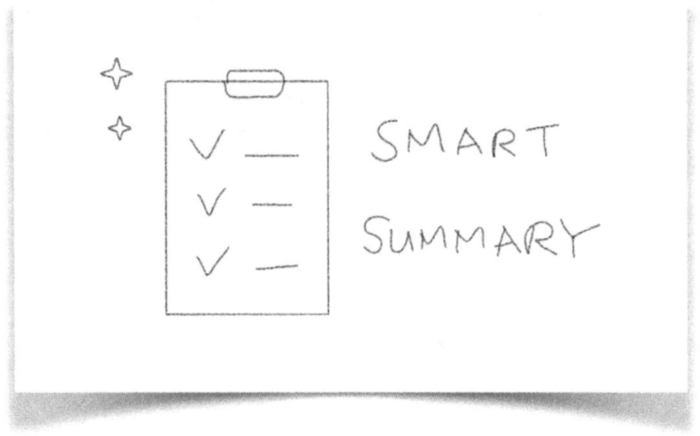

Simple Example

Interviewer: What would be a book you've recently read that's changed the way you think and view the world?

You: I'm an avid reader of many diverse genres. One recent book I found particularly interesting was *Sapiens*, written by Yuval Noah Harrari, a noted historian. The book's thesis is that our human ability to create and share complex fictional narratives, such as religions, mythologies and ideologies has enabled sapiens (humans) to cooperate effectively on a large scale, leading to the rise of civilizations, empires and global systems today. Harrari's book is supported by three main arguments centered around periods of revolution. The first revolution is a cognitive revolution, which involved language and communication of complex ideas. The second revolution is the agricultural revolution allowing for population growth and complex social structure. The third revolution is the scientific revolution, which has led to technological advancements and a paradigm shift from traditional and religious belief systems to a more science- and evidence-based belief system utilizing technology and data.

75. Go With The Cashflows

Simple Strategy

Thinking in terms of cashflows is a crucial skill for many jobs, both within and outside the financial sector. Without money, there would be very few goods or services circulating around the world. Being able to talk about money in a nuanced way — weaved into your job negotiation — demonstrates your ability to understand the financial health of the economy or a specific company and make informed financial decisions. Even if your core job role doesn't directly involve cashflows, arguably many jobs involve cashflows indirectly. Even nonprofits need money to make a positive impact. So, it's an advantage to show you have some exposure to three main cashflow-related concepts. The first is *Operating Cashflows*, which represent the cash generated or used by the organization's core operations (excluding investments and financing activities). The second is *Investing Cashflows*, which represent the cash used to acquire or dispose of long-term assets, such as property, manufacturing and equipment. The third is *Financing Cashflows*, which represent the cash raised or repaid from financing activities, such as issuing or repurchasing stock or borrowing or repaying debt (loans and/or bonds). Also make it a point to scan the business and financial news on a daily basis — even if it's just the headlines — so you have a general idea of financial events surrounding you. Talking about cashflows and in money terms, when needed, will separate you from the (non-money minded) pack.

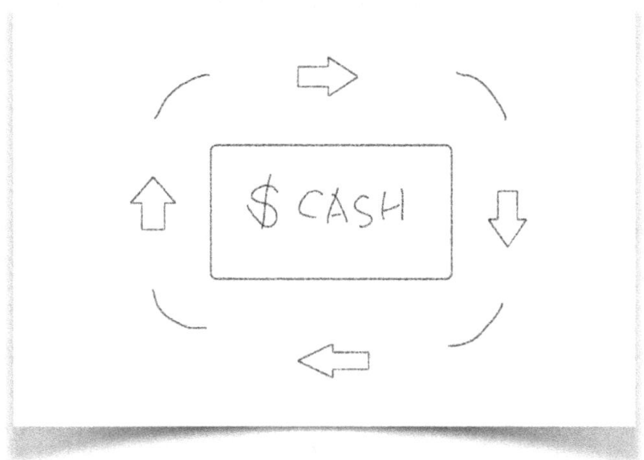

Simple Example

Key Cashflow Concepts:

* The difference between net income and free cashflow

* How cashflows impact a company's valuation

* Key cashflow metrics that are important to an organization

* How cashflows inform investment decisions

76. Dealing With Dirty Tactics

Simple Strategy

Job negotiations can involve high stakes and pressure. You may experience situations where your job interview counterparty tries to use a plethora of tactics to get a sense of whether you can keep calm and carry on — or break under pressure. These tactics can range from subtle pressure to outright deception. It's important to recognize and counter these tactics effectively. The first step is to recognize the dirty tactic. Various types of dirty tactics exist. One dirty tactic is *lowballing.* This is when the employer knowingly offers you a salary or compensation package that's much lower than your expectations or market value, with the hope that you accept it. Putting *extreme time pressure* on you is another dirty tactic. Here, the employer may purposely try to rush you during the negotiation process, pressuring you to make a decision before you've had a chance to fully consider all your options. Yet another dirty tactic involves *personal attacks or threats.* Examples include the employer threatening to rescind your offer or threatening to walk away if you don't agree to its terms, even if it doesn't reflect your true worth. Fight the temptation to defend yourself by using dirty tactics of your own in response — rise above it. Use non-dirty, yet equally effective, tactics to fight against dirty tactics thrown against you.

Simple Example

Clean Tactics to Fight Dirty Tactics

Lowball offer: politely decline the offer and explain that it's below your expectations. Counter with your own salary range, supported by research and evidence.

Time limitations: inform the employer that you need more time to consider the offer and to make an informed decision. Ask, not *if*, but *how long* the employer is willing to extend the deadline.

Personal attacks: remain professional and don't engage in personal attacks. Change the subject back to the negotiation or politely excuse yourself from the conversation. You may also want to cite the incident to senior management or HR.

Threats or ultimatums: calmly inform the employer that threats or ultimatums aren't acceptable and that you'll not be pressured into making a decision under such conditions. Reiterate your interest in the position and your desire to reach a fair agreement. Similar to the case with personal attacks, you may also want to note the incident to senior management or HR.

77. Leverage Logrolling

Simple Strategy

Logrolling is a negotiation technique that involves swapping things that are less important to you for things that may be more important for your Manager or Interviewer. Logrolling often involves an "if-then" proposition or statement. It's a valuable tool in job negotiations because logrolling allows both parties to reach an agreement — with each side able to claim victory. The first step in logrolling is to identify your priorities to determine what's most important to you in a job offer. Consider ranking the following factors: salary, benefits, vacation time, work-life balance, working remotely and bonus. The next step is to estimate what may be important for your Manager or Interviewer. After doing this, identity possible trade-off scenarios for concessions utilizing logrolling. As an example, you may be willing to accept slightly less salary, if your Manager or Interviewer agrees to a more flexible work-from-home (WFH) arrangement.

Simple Example

Interviewer: We're committed to investing in our employees' growth, and we typically offer annual raises of 3-5% year-on-year based on a starting salary of $110,000. We'd also be amenable to considering you for promotion to a more senior position within two years of your starting date, which would potentially come with a significant salary increase.

You: I appreciate what you just mentioned, which are potentially promising career development opportunities. I'm still not quite ready to agree to the original salary that was offered, but I'm willing to consider a compromise. How about we first agree on a salary of $110,000 for the first year, and then $120,000 for the second year, provided I can work remotely two days a week?

Interviewer: That figure sounds reasonable. You should know we're also willing to commit to a performance-based bonus structure that could increase your annual earnings by up to 10% for your first year based on performance.

You: In principle, that sounds like something I could find agreeable. Thank you for your flexibility.

78. Silence Is A Wordless Weapon

Simple Strategy

Silence can be socially uncomfortable. For this reason, people tend to fill silence with words. The strategy here is to flip the silence script. Use silence, at strategic times, as your golden weapon. Silence — paired with purposeful pauses — gives you time to gather your thoughts and formulate responses. Silence also helps you project confidence, while giving you the upper hand in setting the tone and pace of your job negotiation. Because of the social norm to fill silence with words, utilizing silence and purposeful pauses can create a unique situation where the Interviewer is interviewing against him- or herself. This can then lead to improved counteroffers so you can get closer to landing your dream job and getting your worth.

Simple Example

Interviewer: We're willing to offer you a starting salary of $97,000 and a performance-based bonus structure that could increase your annual earnings by up to 10% based on certain performance metrics.

You (*using strategic silence — instead of rushing to reply — to give time to thoughtfully consider the revised offer*)**:** I appreciate your willingness to negotiate on this point. I'm open to your proposal, but I would also like to discuss the possibility of flexible work arrangements.

Interviewer (*pausing briefly*)**:** We value work-life balance and are open to discussing flexible work arrangements. How about working remotely one day per week?

You (*pausing purposely again to carefully evaluate the offer*)**:** Working remotely one day per week would be a net positive from my perspective. So, I'm open to that arrangement, and I'm confident that I can maintain or even boost my productivity while working both remotely and in-person at the office.

79. What If I'm Insulted?

Simple Strategy

Have you ever felt insulted enough to walkout in a job or salary negotiation? Rather than *react* (emotionally), the better strategy is to *respond* (rationally). Walking out when you're highly emotional signals that you've lost control in the negotiation. But if you're able to leave the table in a calm manner, it'll signal that you're still in control (and have mental grit).

Simple Example

The hiring manager suggests you're lucky just to have the opportunity to interview with them, since they typically only recruit from "top-tier" schools and organizations.

Hardball Recruiter: I think you're only minimally qualified for the job. Applicants like you are plentiful and a dime a dozen. So, I'm unsure if it's even worthwhile to continue discussing the position with you given your relatively unremarkable background.

(Emotional) *Reaction*

You: How dare you say that to me?! That's outrageous...I'm out of here (as you stand up, march out, and slam the door behind you)!

(Strategic) *Response*

You: From my perspective, it's quite regretful that you feel this way, despite knowing very little about me. I believe I bring a lot of value to the table. But unfortunately, based on what you just said, I've decided not to proceed further with this interview. I also now know what type of people this organization represents. So, thank you for sharing your perspective, which I'll also be happy to share if asked by any of my fellow peers in the industry.

80. Create Confidence By Curated Communication

Simple Strategy

All words are not created equal. Studies show that certain words matter more than others in projecting confidence, which is essential in any job negotiation. The default strategy, unless your target industry or sector does otherwise, is to use simple words paired with short sentences. Simplicity is elegance. To KISS (Keep It Short and Simple) and tell is a job negotiation virtue. Use sentences with a simple *subject-verb-object* structure, to ensure everything is easy to understand. For your Interviewer to be persuaded to hire you, he or she must first understand what you're trying to say. So, make your words purpose-driven and punchy, which will increase your persuasiveness. Remember, you're not presenting a Nobel Prize winning paper for a group of scholars. You're trying to get a job or promotion. Adam Grant, an organizational psychology professor at The Wharton School of Finance, suggests using definitive language, such as "certainly," "absolutely" and "conclusively" to project knowledge, expertise and confidence. In other words, avoid hedging words, such as "perhaps," "maybe" or "on the one hand" to increase your persuasiveness. These words often convey a lack of confidence. Finally, eliminate filler words, such as "um," "ah" and "well." Popular podcasts edit these filler words for a simple reason: because filler words lower the quality of the overall message and can bore the audience. Apply the same approach and editorialize your chosen message. To ensure you're doing this, do an audio audit. Record yourself using your smartphone's audio app (or other device) in a mock interview setting and see if you use definite (power) words using short sentences with few filler words. You want your audience to be hooked on your every word. So go ahead — KISS and tell.

Simple Example

I'm *confident* that my experience and skills are a *perfect* match for the role.

or

I'm *certainly* a highly motivated and results-oriented worker.

or

Hiring me is *absolutely* the *best* choice you can make.

81. There's No Problems (Only Challenges)

Simple Strategy

The words you use reflect your mindset. To reflect a mindset of getting the job done, use the word "challenge" or "opportunity" — instead of "problem" — during your job negotiations. Such purposefully positively-framed word choices convey a more positive and proactive approach when confronting potential obstacles at work. This type of word reframe and mindset shift also shows you're not intimidated by difficulties, but see them as opportunities for growth and development. It conveys that you're not looking for excuses or ways to shift blame. You're seeking solutions and pathways for iterative improvement. This technique also demonstrates problem-solving potential and a proactive and positive attitude, in which you're not discouraged by setbacks, but find setbacks as motivators to find workable solutions. Overall, using word reframes will reflect a propensity towards personal growth and professional development, which organizations value.

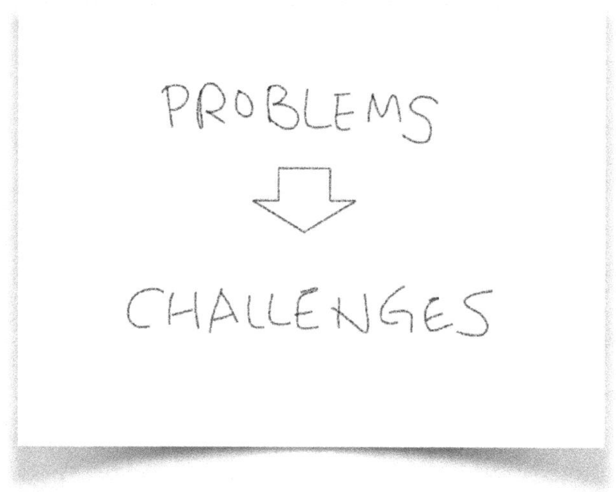

Simple Example

Don't say: I'm concerned about the high turnover rate in the Firm.

Say this instead: I see the turnover rate as a *challenge* to identify and address any underlying issues that may be affecting employee retention.

Don't say: The long working hours are a major problem.

Say this instead: Striving for a healthy work-life balance is a *challenge* I look forward to positively addressing as an invaluable member of your team.

82. Flip The Tables (With Role Reversal)

Simple Strategy

You may encounter a situation where an outlandish demand or first offer is given to you in a job negotiation. As part of your toolbox, use a ninja-like technique known as *role reversal*. This technique involves using words, such as "If you were in my shoes, would you accept the offer you just gave me?" It puts your Interviewer or current management to see things from your vantage point, not just their own. Role reversal is a powerful tool that can be used in job negotiations to give your potential employer a deeper understanding of your perspective, which will strengthen your own negotiation position. By effectively using role reversal in job negotiation settings, your potential employer will gain a deeper understanding of your perspective (beyond its own perspective), build trust faster and create paths to identify common ground.

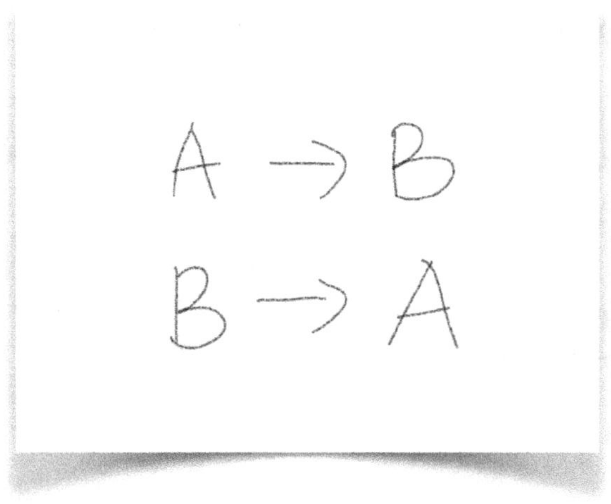

Simple Example

Current Manager: I'm prepared to offer you a 1% salary increase for the next fiscal year.

You: *If you were in my shoes* — given that inflation exceeded 5% this fiscal year — would you accept a salary increase of only 1% — which effectively represents taking a significant pay *cut* (which is the exact opposite of a pay increase)?

83. Nodding Isn't Necessarily Needed

Simple Strategy

During a job negotiation, you may feel the need to please. Part of this pleasing pivot may include conscious or unconscious head nodding. Although nodding or tilting your head may seem like a harmless gesture, it can actually have a significant impact on how you're being perceived in a job negotiation. Some nodding is useful. But nodding too much isn't necessarily needed — or helpful to securing a job offer. Studies have shown that nodding is often associated with agreement and approval — even if your intention is *not* to agree, but to simply signal that you're actively listening. By trying to decrease the amount of times you nod or tilt your head, you minimize the risk of unconscious biases influencing the negotiation. Nodding or tilting your head can also sometimes be perceived as fidgeting or nervousness. Maintaining a neutral head position projects a thoughtful, composed and confident demeanor, which can be crucial in establishing a favorable impression in your job interview.

Simple Example

Instead of nodding when the employer expresses a preference for a particular salary range, maintain a neutral head position, and politely yet clearly and confidently, express your desired salary range, explaining your rationale for each deal point.

84. The Downsides Of Upward Intonation

Simple Strategy

You may not realize when you use upward intonations —
which occurs when the pitch and tone of your voice goes up —
when ending your sentences. Doing this may seem like it
should be inconsequential. But on the contrary, using upward
intonations can have tangible negative repercussions. First,
upward intonations make your statements sound less
definitive and more uncertain, when stating your opinions or
preferences. This can raise doubts about your conviction and
expertise, potentially weakening your negotiation position.
Upward intonation can also make your statements sound less
forceful, reducing their persuasive impact. Upward intonation
can also make you sound less confident in your abilities and
confidence, undermining your authority as a Job Candidate.
Another consequence of upward intonation is that it could be
associated with deference, subservience and a need for
approval, which can all be detrimental to getting your worth.
Instead, use statements with downward intonation since they
are generally perceived as more persuasive, confident and
convincing.

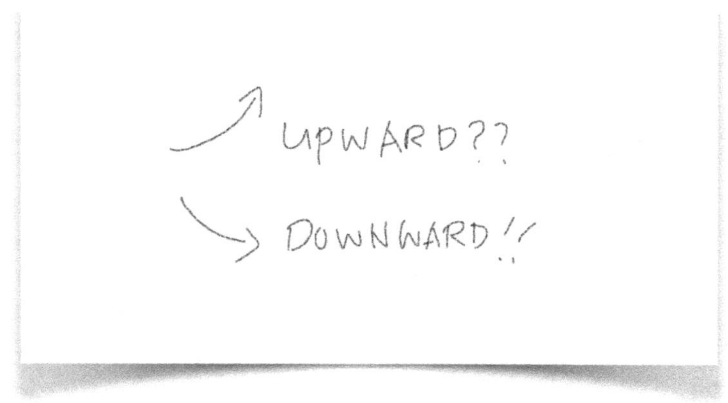

Simple Example

Practice downward intonation: consciously practice using sentences with downward intonation at the end, especially when making statements about your skills, experience or desired outcomes.

Combine downward intonation with other nonverbal cues of confidence: examples include maintaining eye contact, using open body language and speaking at a moderate pace.

85. Work Your Walkaways (To Saying Yes)

Simple Strategy

Let's say you receive an offer during a job negotiation. Should you accept it or not? One framework to get to the answer is to consider your alternatives to saying yes to the job offer. First, decide on your best walkaway alternative — referred to as your BATNA (Best Alternative To a Negotiated Agreement). The objective here is to analyze and find your *best* alternative (BATNA), among all your yesable alternatives. Next, compare the job offer to your BATNA. If your job offer is better than your BATNA, it's one indicator to say yes. But if not, then say no to the job offer (and say yes to your BATNA). Thinking about your walkaway alternatives — especially your BATNA — will help you to boost your negotiation power during your next job negotiation.

Simple Example

* You're negotiating your starting salary for a new job offer.
  Your desired salary is $75,000 per year, but Firm A's offer is
  only $70,000.

* You decide you have several "yesable" walkaway alternatives
  to Firm A's $70,000 offer.

* BATNA: an offer from Firm B for $65,000 (including
  benefits, such as full health benefits, a partial week remote
  work option and pet insurance).

* Based on your set of standards, you weigh Firm A's offer
  ($70,000 with minimal benefits) against your BATNA (Firm
  B's offer of $65,000 *plus its non-monetary benefits*).

* You determine that your overall BATNA (Firm B's offer) is
  better than Firm A's offer (based on salary and benefits
  combined).

* You accept Firm B's offer (say yes to your BATNA) and reject
  Firm A's offer.

86. Power Of A Principled No

Simple Strategy

As a social species, people are generally socially conditioned to say yes. Certain Interviewers may use this to get what they want, at your expense. Being aware of this is half the battle. Knowledge is power. So, pair this knowledge with the following key simple strategy: a principled no can trump a weak yes. *A principled no* is when you say no to an offer because it isn't giving you what you want. But to get what you want, you must know what you want — not broadly, but exactly. Believe it or not, many fall victim to saying yes due to social conditioning by accepting a subpar starting package. This is known as a *weak yes*. Before giving your reply, ask yourself, "Why would I say yes to something that doesn't get me what I want?" Knowing what you want before — not during or after — your job negotiation process will help you know whether a principled no is your best power move. After giving a principled no, you could seek other opportunities that potentially give you what you want. A principled no, in certain conditions, also gives time for an organization to provide a better counteroffer closer to, at or exceeding what you originally wanted.

Simple Example

Interviewer: I'd like to provide you a salary offer of $115,000 to work from our Chicago branch.

You: I think we're very close to agreeable terms. If we can just adjust the salary figure to a reasonable range between $130,000 to $140,000 working from the Firm's New York headquarters (rather than from Chicago), then I'd be happy to say yes.

Interviewer: I'm going to be honest. This is a "take it or leave it" proposition.

You: If that's the case, I regret to say that I'm unable to accept the offer based on its current terms. Thank you, however, for your time and consideration throughout the interview process.

87. Interview Like A Star

Simple Strategy

People fear job negotiations because of the unknown. One great unknown is the type of interview questions that could potentially be asked. Broadly speaking, three types of interview questions exist. The first type is a *situational interview question*, where you're placed in a hypothetical situation. The second type is a *behavioral interview question*, where you're asked to share examples of scenarios and explanations based on situations you were in professionally. A question phrased in terms of "Tell me about a time when..." is an example of a behavioral question. The third type is a *competency interview question*, where you're judged on your ability to fill specific skills. One way of dealing with these interview question types is by using the STAR method (Situation, Task, Action, Result).

Simple Example

Interviewer: Tell me about a time you had to work under extreme time pressure.

You: Sure, I'd be happy to answer that question. Let me break down my answer into several parts, specifically in terms of Situation, Task, Action and Results.

Situation (S): I was working as a sales associate at a clothing store during the holiday season. It was the busiest time of the year.

Task (T): My task was to provide high-quality customer service and to process transactions quickly, correctly and efficiently.

Action (A): I prioritized the most urgent tasks and delegated some of the less critical ones to my colleagues. I also used effective communication skills to greet customers, answer their questions and handle any complaints or issues during our most busy season. I maintained a positive and professional attitude throughout the duration of my duties.

Result (R): I was able to serve a high volume of customers and also achieve my sales targets. I also received positive feedback from my manager and customers for my performance. I learned how to work efficiently and calmly under pressure — all skills and traits that I believe can be effectively leveraged towards the position I'm interviewing for now.

88. Your (Final) Magic Interview Question

Simple Strategy

It's fairly common for your Interview Panel to ask whether you have questions for them at the end of the interview. Your first few questions may be fairly routine questions, such as asking about next steps or expectations (but not salary, unless asked). But what should be your *last* question? Based on research by a leading social psychologist, Robert Cialdini, your final magic question should be, "What aspects of my background and qualifications would lead you to choose me over your other Candidates?" By asking this one question, you're strategically accomplishing several things at once. First, the Interviewer is tasked with mentally reframing you as "the chosen one" — rather than simply just another Job Candidate. Second, by asking this strategic question, the Interviewer is put in a position as your advocate and ally. Third, your Interviewer's response to your final question will give you invaluable inside information for further stages of the job negotiation. This strategy takes the adage, "ask and you shall receive" to the next level.

Simple Example

Interviewer: So, do you have any final questions for us?

You: Yes, I do. What aspects of my background and qualifications would lead you to choose me over your other Candidates?

Interviewer: That's a good question that I've honestly very rarely encountered before. Let me see. Well, I'd say you have the right expertise and experience for the job. And if anything, we know that you ask creative questions that could lead to innovative solutions. These are all traits that we seek and need for our organization. I'm sure there would be other additional reasons to hire you as well, since it appears you're confident, curious and a consummate learner.

Part 3: After The Job Interview

89. Be A Fan Of Follow-Ups

Simple Strategy

After your job interview, you may think you're done swaying for maximum pay. But don't let your guard down too early. There's still the follow-through to get you past the finish line. One post-interview follow-through technique is to send thank you emails to your Interviewers. Sending thank you emails, in a format that fits your industry, has several advantages. First, it underscores your communication skills and professionalism. One field experiment study showed that thank you messages can measurably improve a Job Candidate's rating on key evaluation criteria. Second, a sincere expression of appreciation shows the employer your gratitude for their time and consideration, fostering potentially positive feelings towards you compared to other Job Candidates. Third, a thank you message reflects your continued interest in the position and that you want the communication lines to remain open. This can be beneficial for future discussions or negotiations, even if you don't get an offer this time around. Overall, sending a thank you message after your job negotiation is a simple gesture with significant potential benefits. It's a valuable tool for enhancing communication, expressing gratitude and ultimately improving your job search and hiring potential. So, it pays to say "thank you."

Simple Example

Dear Ms. Guerrara (Hiring Manager),

I truly appreciate your time and consideration throughout the interview and process. Your willingness to discuss the position, given your busy schedule, is testament to your commitment to creating a positive and supportive work environment for the Firm.

I am confident that I can make a significant contribution to the Firm and am eager to begin learning and growing in this role. Please let me know what the next steps are in the interview process.

Thank you again for this opportunity. I look forward to joining your organization soon.

Sincerely,
Norah Lee

90. Think In Specific Money Terms

Simple Strategy

Let's face it. Money makes things happen. So, you need to make money happen. To think clearly about money, think about specific monetary "deal points" that are important to you. Then rank order them in terms of importance to you. Salary is probably the big ticket item when it comes to money matters. But remember: bonuses, 401(k)/IRA contributions, titles and health insurance are also important to think about in money terms during a job negotiation.

Simple Example

* **Salary**: $150,000 (your ideal point, known as your Aspiration Point)

* **Bonus**: $30,000 (20% of your Salary), guaranteed for the first two years of employment; thereafter performance-based

* **401(k) / IRA Contributions**: Firm will match your contributions up to $20,000 annually

* **Health Insurance**: 100% covered for you and your family members, including medical, dental, vision and pet insurance

91. Focus On Total Compensation

Simple Strategy

While money makes the world go round — believe it or not —
things other than money also matter in your job negotiations.
What you're looking for from a successful job negotiation may
not always be the most money. Instead, what you're looking for
is the best *overall* job offer package for the position. Non-
money matters include (but aren't limited to) your
position/title, duties/responsibilities, vacation days, sick days,
city/location and work from home (WFH) option. Don't just
seek the most salary. It's just one piece of the puzzle. Widen
your lens' aperture to wide angle mode to strategically focus on
the entire landscape.

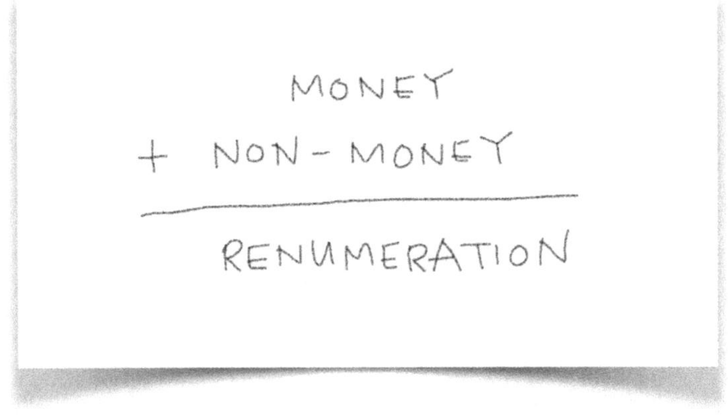

Simple Example

Starting Package Terms and Conditions

* **Position/Title**: Senior Associate

* **Duties/Responsibilities**: Lead in valuations of emerging market debt instruments / Supervise analysts / Liaised between vice presidents and analysts for emerging markets team

* **Paid Vacation Days**: 17 (business) days (annual)

* **Paid Sick Days**: 5 (business) days (annual)

* **City/Location**: San Francisco, California, with the option to transfer to another location in two years

* **WFH**: Option to work remotely for two (business) days per week

92. Job Interviews Are Personal (But Don't Take It Personally)

Simple Strategy

Let's face it: applying for jobs gets personal. You disclose personal aspects about your education, past and current work experience as well as skills, interests and aspirations. For some people, this may seem like a process that's very personal. But behind the fancy titles and positions are human beings like you and me. Human decision-makers are both *logical* and *biological.* This means decisions are driven by both logic and emotions. As your interview strategy, appeal to both the logical and emotional side of your Interviewers. The Logicians will want cost-benefit analysis and rational factors. On the other hand, Humanists will want to see that you're not just a walking calculator, but also someone who has warmth as well as competence. After the job interview process, if you don't get the offer, don't take it personally. There's so many variables and considerations that can ebb and flow throughout the hiring process. You can't control the outcome. But you can control the process underlying the outcome. Focus on the process (controllables), not the outcome (uncontrollables).

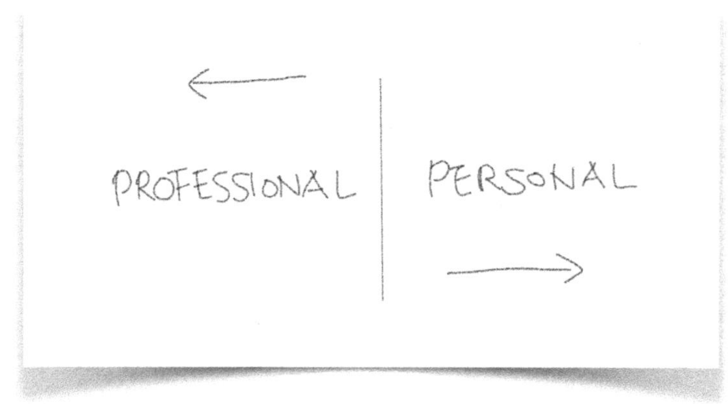

Simple Example

Instead of letting discouragement take hold, approach your job journey with resilience:

* **Self-reflection**: After each rejection, take time to analyze the feedback (if provided) or reflect on the interview process.

* **Ask yourself**: Were there any areas where I could have improved my presentation? Does this organization's culture seem like a good fit for me?

* **Learning from setbacks**: View rejections as opportunities to learn and refine your interview skills, portfolio presentation or tailor your resume (CV) to specific roles.

* **Maintaining a positive attitude**: Finding the perfect job takes time and effort. It's not an instance process. Stay positive by focusing on the progress made and celebrating small wins, like getting shortlisted for an interview.

* **Networking and learning**: Use this time to network with professionals in your field. Attend industry events, connect with designers on LinkedIn and explore online courses to keep your skills sharp.

* **Focusing on the journey**: Don't let job rejections influence your self-worth. Maintain a healthy work-life balance. Engage in hobbies and activities you enjoy and stay motivated and energized. There's no such thing as failure. There's only feedback towards success.

93. Practice (Post-Interview) Positivity

Simple Strategy

After a job interview, you may experience a whirlwind of emotions. Some may feel like they nailed the interview, while others may overly focus on "what ifs." It may seem obvious to say, but it's often overlooked: you can't change the past. And there's nothing gained from crying over spilled milk. It's already behind you. What you can control are the controllables. One important controllable is to practice post-interview positivity. Our brains tend to have a negativity bias. So being positive requires intentional countervailing acts to overcome our negative biases. One way to stay positive is to ask yourself, "What's the worst that can happen after the interview?" You can either get the job or not. If you get the job, that's great. But if you don't get the job, you're in exactly the same spot as you were before your interview. In other words, nothing ventured, nothing gained. Not even the greatest players can hit a home run on every swing. True failure is not swinging at all. You don't want to spend your life just watching balls whiz by you without swinging for success. Another thought to keep things positive is to ask yourself, "What have I learned from the interview to increase my chances for success in the future?" Make a list of three to five interview takeaways for constant self-improvement. This is what separates the best from the rest. Finally, say to yourself, "Well, in a way, the interview was like an intense networking session." During the interview, you met exactly the type of people in your target industry. Did you like them? Did you want to emulate them? How did they think? How did they talk? How did they analyze information? How did they carry themselves? Exposure to such career benchmark professionals is priceless. So, treat it as exactly that: a precious and priceless part of the process.

Simple Example

Ask yourself: What have I learned from the interview to increase my chances for success in the future?

Make a list of three to five interview lessons learned for constant self-improvement

94. Use Positive Pep Talk (To Yourself)

Simple Strategy

Positive self-talk has been shown to have many benefits for increased performance. One study found that positive self-talk led to better performance by athletes when it came to motor tasks. Another study found that positive self-talk was one of the most effective ways to improve academic achievement. Positive pep talk increases motivation, such as by saying, "I can do this if I keep trying" (rather than "I'm never going to be able to do this"). It also reduces anxiety by focusing on your strengths, such as saying, "I've spoken successfully in interviews before, and I'm confident I'll be able to do it again." Positive self-talk also helps with improved attention, such as by focusing on steps for success (rather than thinking about missteps leading to failure). It also enhances confidence by reminding yourself of past successes and instances of your demonstrated resilience, such as saying to yourself, "I've got this" (instead of, "I'm not good enough for this job"). Some studies also suggest that framing positive self-talk in the third person may also be beneficial, such as by saying "You've got this!" or "You'd be awesome at this job!"

Simple Example

* **Avoid saying:** I'm not going to get this job.

* **Say this instead:** I'm a highly-qualified Job Candidate for this job. I can't wait to show the Interviewer why I'd be great for the role!

* **Avoid saying:** I'm so nervous about this interview.

* **Say this instead:** I've prepared as well for this interview as anyone could. I've got this!

* **Avoid saying:** I'm not sure if I'm qualified for the job.

* **Say this instead:** I have all the requisite skills and experience that the position is seeking. I'm going to highlight my amazing strengths and accomplishments and nail the interview!

95. Every Word Matters (In Your Employment Contract)

Simple Strategy

The end of the interview is not the end of the interview process. As the adage goes, "The devil is in the details." During the interview stage, you likely only agreed on big picture terms and conditions, such as your overall compensation package and title. But now you have to get down to the next stage of your interview process: your legally-binding employment contract. During this stage, make sure to trust but verify what you're being told. Remember: the best advocate for you is you. As one case in point, even if you're told the contract is "standard for everyone," "pro forma" or even "non-negotiable," you can still potentially exercise influence in reshaping it to a final agreed-upon version that's acceptable to you. The first step is to make sure your big ticket items are true and correct, such as salary, position, work location, health benefits, bonuses, remote work options and paid vacation. The second step is to focus on the small but important ticket items, such as sick/bereavement leave, promotion reviews and termination clauses. These contract terms will usually last throughout your time with your organization, whether it's for a day or a decade. So, make sure each term is acceptable to you now and for your foreseeable tenure with the organization. If any terms aren't acceptable, don't sign the contract — reengage with your employer — and ask that it be changed. Don't be afraid to fight for your value. (And if you still have legal questions, read my book, *American Law 101: An Easy Primer on the U.S. Legal System*).

Simple Example

- Initial Offer

Salary: $85,000 per year
Benefits: Standard health insurance plan, 2 weeks annual vacation
Start Date: Monday, May 1st
Termination Clause: At-will employment (for any reason)

- Candidate (John) Initiates Negotiations

Salary: John requests a salary of $90,000, citing his relevant experience and skills.
Benefits: John requests a more comprehensive health insurance plan with additional coverage for dental and vision coverage.

Start Date: John asks for a later start date of June 1st due to previous personal commitments.

Termination Clause: John requests a clause outlining specific reasons for termination to protect him from unfair dismissal.

- Company's Counteroffer

Salary: $87,000 per year, with a performance review after 6 months for a potential salary increase.

Benefits: Standard health insurance plan with an option to upgrade at an additional cost.

Start Date: May 15th

Termination Clause: At-will employment, with 2 weeks notice required for termination from either party.

- Final Agreement

Salary: $87,500 per year, with a performance review after 6 months for potential salary increase.

Benefits: Standard health insurance plan with an additional $50 monthly contribution by the Firm towards higher premium costs for more comprehensive coverage.

Start Date: May 22nd

Termination Clause: At-will employment, with 2 weeks written notice required for termination from either party.

96. (Almost) Always Ask For More

Simple Strategy

After several rounds of interviews, the moment of truth arrives. The Interviewer says the Firm is willing to give you an offer — she then writes the magic number on a piece of paper — and then slides the figure to you across the desk (for dramatic effect). You're happy that you're getting an offer. But when you look at the number, you're disappointed because it's below what you expected. So what should you do?: (a) be the so-called team player and take one for the team, accepting the low offer; or (b) risk creating an awkward situation by asking for more? The answer is: you should generally ask for more — if your value isn't reflected in the offer. Some employers will purposely use a lowball tactic in the hope that you'll accept a number that's close (but below) a reasonable figure. Others may give you a number based on flawed information, biases and misperceptions. In fact, one seminal study by a notable researcher, Linda Babcock, found that women were much *less* likely to ask for more money than men, widening the gender pay gap. If you believe the offer meets your expectations, you could accept it. But if you feel like you're being undervalued, draw a line in the sand and stand your ground to get your worth.

Simple Example

You: Based on my research and experience, I believe a salary closer to $120,000 would be more appropriate.

Hiring Manager: I understand your perspective. However, our budget for this position is $105,000. Is there anything else we can do to make the offer more attractive?

You: I'm open to discussing additional benefits, such as a signing bonus or more vacation time. I'm also particularly interested in the opportunity to work on projects involving technology or other areas in my expertise. How can we discuss potential ways to incorporate these into the offer?

Hiring Manager: I think we should certainly be able to accommodate some of your requests. I remain optimistic, so let me get back to you regarding a possible confirmation on the points you raised.

97. Use Expected Value (To Choose Between Job Offers)

Simple Strategy

Let's say you find yourself in a dream scenario: you have two potential job offers at the same time: Offer 1 and Offer 2. How do you decide which one to accept? One framework to get to the answer is called Expected Value (EV). It's a fundamental concept in probability and decision theory that helps people make informed choices under uncertainty (without full information). In the context of job negotiations, Expected Value can be a valuable tool for evaluating different job offers and making decisions that align with your long-term career goals. To use Expected Value in your job negotiations, estimate the likelihood of receiving each job offer in terms of a probability (an educated guess). Then multiply that number with each job offer's overall estimated value (a figure that incorporates all monetary and non-monetary amounts). By using Expected Value, you should choose the job offer with the highest expected value (everything else being equal).

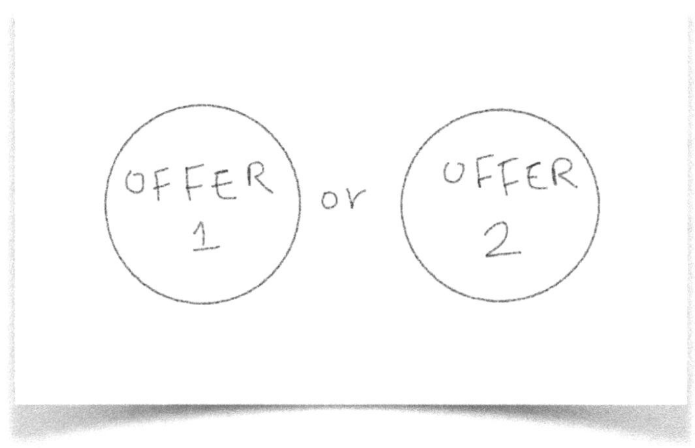

Simple Example

You have two job offers below (at this stage, assume only ranges have been provided to you): Offer 1 and Offer 2. Apply Expected Value (EV = % x $)

Offer A:
Salary: $80,000
Benefits: Standard benefits package
Work-life balance: Demanding schedule, limited flexibility
Career development: Limited opportunities for advancement

Offer B:
Salary: $75,000
Benefits: Excellent benefits package, including generous vacation time and health insurance

Work-life balance: Flexible schedule, work-from-home options

Career development: Strong opportunities for growth and promotion

- **STEP 1:** To evaluate these offers using EV, assign probabilities to each offer and determine the value of each outcome

<u>Offer A:</u>

Probability: 0.6 (60% chance of receiving the offer terms)

Value: $80,000 (salary) + $10,000 (intangible benefits) = $90,000

Offer A EV: 0.6 x $90,000 = **$54,000**

<u>Offer B:</u>

Probability: 0.7 (70% chance of receiving the offer terms)

Value: $75,000 (salary) + $20,000 (intangible benefits) = $95,000

Calculate the expected value for each offer:

Offer B EV: 0.7 x $95,000 = **$66,500**

- **STEP 2**: Offer A ($54,000) < Offer B ($66,500), including salary and non-salary benefits.

Using Expected Value, Offer B has a higher expected value based on the given inputs (combination of a strong benefits package, flexible work-life balance, and promising career development opportunities).

98. When To Use Recruiters

Simple Strategy

When do you know when it's time to use a recruiter? A general rule of thumb is that the more experience you have in the industry, the more advantageous recruiters can be for you. If you're a recent graduate, or junior in rank, then not using a recruiter and applying directly to your chosen industry or organization may be the best (and sometimes only) option. But if you have work experience and/or expertise, then utilizing a recruiter may be a great option. The advantages of using recruiters are their access to a large potential pipeline of organizations and hiring managers, which can increase your chances of securing an interview. Recruiters also can save you time by getting you past initial screening processes, which can save you time and effort. Recruiters can also provide actionable advice, which can help present you to other organizations in the best possible light. Finally, recruiters can help, and even be the main point of contact and advocate-negotiator, for your salary and benefits packages. Recruiters tend to be specialists who focus on specific areas and industries. So, find the recruiter that best matches your target job or industry. You can contact recruiters directly through their organization's website or LinkedIn. Finally, the use of recruiters has some downsides. Namely, recruiters typically get paid for their services in the form of a fee that's taken from your negotiated salary and/or your hiring organization's budget.

YOU → RECRUITER

Simple Example

Consider your target industry: in some industries, such as finance or technology, it's more common to use recruiters. In other industries, such as education or healthcare, it's more common practice to apply directly.

Evaluate your experience level: if you're a recent graduate or have limited work experience, a recruiter may not be able to effectively help you in your job search. If you have more experience, you may be more successful using a recruiter.

Research specific roles: look for job postings that explicitly mention whether applications directly from Job Candidates or recruiters are accepted.

99. After Getting Hired, Get Laid Off

Simple Strategy

One career strategy is to move jobs every two to three years, if you're relatively young and new in your career. The thinking is that staying the same means being a step behind, as the world moves forward as you stay in place at your job. Stagnation is the kiss of career death. After getting hired, stay long enough, but not too long (unless you're on the fast track in a particular organization). When deciding to leave and look for career opportunities elsewhere, remember that quitting isn't your only option. There's another, somewhat counterintuitive option, besides quitting: it's to *get laid off* from your job. So why would you want to purposely get laid off? If you quit or get fired, you're generally not entitled to additional renumeration from your employer. Getting fired also may make it more difficult to receive unemployment benefits. But if you strategically get laid off — by pre-emptively negotiating with your employer about this option — you could potentially get a *severance package* worth several months or more of your salary. The severance pay you negotiate and receive can then be used for almost anything since it's money in your pocket. Getting laid off and negotiating a severance package can change your career trajectory and what you're able to do with your life. So, after getting hired, don't quit. Strategically structure a severance package by getting laid off.

Simple Example

You: Thank you for taking the time to meet with me about my severance package. I appreciate you outlining the initial terms.

(Take a minute or so to review the offer silently.)

You: I've been with the company for 8 years and I'm proud of the contributions I've made. In reviewing the package, I noticed the severance pay is lower than expected. While I understand the company's position, I'm asking for 17% more based on my successful track record with the company.

Employer: We appreciate your contributions as well. However, our severance package is based on our standard policy.

You: I understand there's a standard policy, but given my past performance, I believe an increased severance, as stated earlier, would be fair compensation for my service and the transition period.

Employer: Okay, I appreciate you being clear with me about what you believe is fair compensation relating to your severance package. Let me speak internally with my colleagues to see if we can come to a mutually-agreeable arrangement based on the terms you mentioned. I'll be in touch soon.

You: Thank you for considering my terms. I'm confident that we can agree on a package that works for both of us, and look forward to hearing from you soon.

100. Always Think Win-Win

Simple Strategy

If you're only thinking in terms of "what's in it for me?" (WIIFM) then you may not be positioning yourself for maximum success. Avoid thinking in terms of your viewpoint only. Think also about the Firm's perspective. For both sides to get to yes, both have to envision a situation where both are better off together than separate. In a situation where both get to yes, each side is taking a bet on each other, among a variety of opportunity costs (other potential employees and/or Job Candidates). Even if you're thinking in terms of "what's in it for *me*?" you should then ask "what's in it for *them*?" (WIIFT). Widen the aperture of your job negotiation lens. It's a two-sided interaction and decision-making process. As the idiom goes, "It takes two to tango." So, before the job negotiation, write a list of skillsets or experience in which the Firm would benefit from hiring you over other similarly-suited employees. Put this list alongside a separate list of specific reasons why choosing Firm A would be more beneficial than choosing Firm B. Adam Grant of the Wharton School of Finance characterizes workers who think only about themselves as Takers, while those who think about others as Givers. In Grant's research, Givers had more long-term success in an organization than Takers. Another maxim states, "To receive, you must give." The takeaway: be a Giver, not a Taker. Knowing this is another tool in your toolbox to create a "win-win" job negotiation — to get your worth — and situate you for long-term career success.

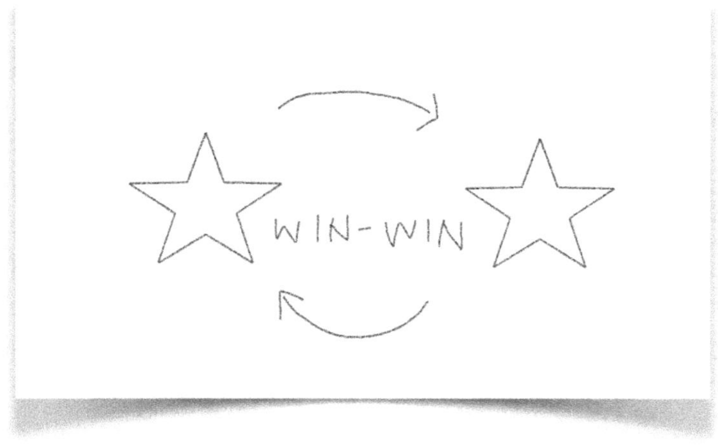

Simple Example

Think: What skillsets and experience do I have to help your organization achieve its objectives?

Don't Think: What's in it for me by joining the organization?

Part 4: Bonus Section

Bonus #1. Craft Your Dream Resume (CV)

Simple Strategy

You've heard of vision boards. They're often used as aspirational target practice to achieve specific objectives, from losing weight to becoming a millionaire. But for those non-believers, don't laugh: studies show that envisioning success helps create success. In this spirit, craft and curate your dream resume (CV). This exercise will help extrapolate the many ideas percolating in your head to specific written (and visualized) targets. Doing this helps create a blueprint for future success in two ways. The first blueprint occurs when you're writing your dream resume (CV). Writing is one exact version extrapolated from your brain's many mental versions. Writing converts cognitive concoctions into reality. The second reinforcing blueprint occurs when you actually look at your dream resume (CV). Seeing is believing. And much like a vision board for success, you should keep referring to your dream version resume (CV) to remind yourself of your exact career targets. In the process, you'll also be able to measure how far, or close, you are to your goals. As the mantra goes, you need to measure what matters. If you don't craft your dream resume (CV), you won't be able to measure — or know — what truly matters.

Simple Example

- Dream Resume (CV)

Education

University of California, Berkeley (Berkeley, CA)
GPA: 3.9 (*summa cum laude*)

Experience

Google, Data Privacy Intern (San Francisco, CA)
OpenAI, AI ethics intern (San Francisco, CA)

Bonus #2. List Impressive References (Who *REALLY* Know You)

Simple Strategy

Some recruiters or job postings will require a Reference List. Don't confuse your Reference List with a "Famous People I Know List." You want References that are both relevant and respectable (Senior Manager, Director, Team Lead) to the job description. You also want your References to be people who know you well. How well should References know you? Think: if you were asked to write a Reference on your own behalf, what exactly would you write about yourself? Would it be compelling or legally bland? The threshold question is: what specific examples, situations or cases could the Reference say about you? You may even want to ask if providing a short summary for the person writing your Reference would be helpful (as a reference point). The more specific, the more helpful to your hiring chances. The more vague, the less helpful. Remember also to ask your References for their permission to be listed as a reference. References could include mentors, advisors, former managers or faculty, to name a few. They should not be your family or friends. The best References are your career cheerleaders — find them and ask them to help you — if they're happy when you ask, you know you've chosen the right Reference.

Simple Example

- Your Resume (CV)

References

Dr. Myra Mendelssohn, Department Chair, University A

Brandon Burk, Managing Partner, Law Firm B

Lizza Livingston, Founder, Nonprofit C

Bonus #3. Be Aesthetically Minimal (Beware Being Blingy)

Simple Strategy

Minimalism is a useful strategy when it comes to accessories, especially if you don't know that much about your target organization's culture or ethos. One study observed that individuals who dressed professionally and conservatively were seen as more competent and trustworthy than those who dressed casually or wore excessive accessories. Other research results confirmed that professional attire and minimal accessories were associated with higher perceptions of likability, competence and employability. In general, it's best to err on the side of caution and minimalism when choosing accessories for your job negotiations. Avoid anything that is overly flashy, distracting or attention-grabbing. The goal is to project a professional and polished image that aligns with the expectations of your target organization (unless your target organizations is less formal, in which case, you should mirror the stylistic sense and sensibilities of those already working for that organization).

Simple Example

For Formal Firm Settings

<u>Men:</u>
Dark suit
Simple watch
Subtle tie or shirt

<u>Women:</u>
Dark suit
Subtle scarf or brooch
Simple earrings or pendant necklace

Bonus #4. Colors Are A Strategy

Simple Strategy

In theory, the colors we wear in a job negotiation should have little or no impact on your job negotiations. In practice, colors are a persuasive nonverbal force. Color can play a subtle yet significant role in job negotiations, influencing perceptions and emotions that can affect the job negotiation outcome. Color can also influence the perception of your confidence and competence as a Job Candidate. It plays a role in conveying trustworthiness and approachability. And it reflects whether you've considered the organization's culture or industry. One study found that those who wore colors associated with confidence and competence, such as navy blue or black, were more likely to achieve favorable job negotiation outcomes. Although color is just one aspect of nonverbal communication, it should be strategically utilized with other nonverbal communication considerations, such as body language, facial expressions, verbal cadence and vocal tone. Colorology may seem to some like astrology. But the difference is that colorology is backed by scientific methodology.

Simple Example

* **Navy blue:** conveys authority, trustworthiness and professionalism

* **Black:** exudes sophistication, power and elegance

* **Gray:** signals intelligence, dependability and neutrality

* **Blue:** projects calmness, trustworthiness and approachability

* **Green:** suggests creativity, growth and sustainability

* **Red:** radiates energy, passion and confidence

* **Yellow:** exudes optimism, friendliness and communication

* **Orange:** conveys enthusiasm, creativity and warmth

Bonus #5. Be Comfortable In Your Interview Attire

Simple Strategy

One key to interview success is to be comfortable and relaxed. One way to be comfortable and relaxed — in an otherwise uncomfortable and formal setting of a job interview — is repetition. Malcolm Gladwell cited 10,000 hours of repetition (practice) were necessary to become a genius (expert). Lots of repetition leads to expertise. Expertise leads to confidence. And confidence translates into comfort and a relaxed state. This type of natural state allows you to perform most optimally. Your Interviewers will sense this confidence and comfort, which in turn, will give them confidence and comfort in hiring you. An act of repetition for career success is to wear your chosen interview attire before your interview day. You don't need to spend 10,000 hours in your interview attire. But you should feel comfortable enough wearing it so that it doesn't make you feel uncomfortable or awkward. Ideally your interview day attire should feel like an extension of your own body. The last thing you want to be thinking during your interview is how tight or loose your interview outfit feels. If it's a new outfit, try to wear it at least a few times before your big day. Even if it's not a new outfit, your existing outfit could need to be dry cleaned or cleaned up. Separately, because every person's contours are different, consider professionally tailoring your suit to fit the specific lines and curves of your body. It may cost you a pretty penny, but it's value is priceless. The real question is: how can you *not* afford to do it? More important than the brand of the suit, is the *fit* of the suit.

Simple Example

Business attire checklist:

* Buy high quality attire that is simple and elegant
* Have a trusted friend or family member give you a second opinion on whether the attire you want to buy is a good choice
* Tailor your attire to your specific lines and curves
* Wear your chosen outfit several times before your interview day

Bonus #6. Know Your Exact Interview Location

Simple Strategy

Reducing the number of uncertainties will keep you calm and boost your confidence for your big interview day. As part of your preparation stage, do a "mock run" of the route you'll take to your interview. If you have time, do this physically (for in-person interviews). If you're in a time crunch, then doing your mock-run through step-by-step directions using Google Maps (or similar app) would be the next best thing. But know that digitally getting to your interview location compared to physically getting there is the difference between theory and practice. As Albert Einstein quipped, "In theory, theory and practice are the same, but in practice, they are different." The takeaway: do a mock run to your interview location, so you don't face the reality of Einstein's quote on your super important interview day.

Simple Example

Mock Run to Interview Site

Google Maps (estimated time): 30 minutes

8:15 am: Leave home to take Uber to interview location

8:30 am: Uber arrives (later than you expected due to unexpected traffic congestion)

9:15 am: Uber arrives to the Interview Site (later than expected due to a traffic accident)

9:30 am: Interview start time

Bonus #7. Sleep Is Key To Success

Simple Strategy

Sleep is your secret weapon. Getting a good eight or nine hours of sleep the night before your big day has several secret advantages. It allows you to think clearly and make sound decisions. It allows you to stay focused and positive. Plenty of sleep also helps you to maximize your overall performance during a job interview. Other benefits include the fact that a good night's rest will reduce your anxiety, boost your energy level and improve your overall first impression appearance. You don't want the very first thought of your Interviewer to be, "Wow, this person looks tired." Instead, you want the Interviewer to instead think, "Wow, this person's looks and sounds sharp — and thinks like a million bucks!" And a million bucks is exactly what you may appear to deserve thanks, in part, to getting sufficient sleep.

Simple Example

Your Possible Evening Schedule (before the interview day)

6:30 pm: Eat an early dinner

7:30 pm: Review your final notes for the interview

8:00 pm: Watch a relaxing movie or TV show (avoid news and social media)

9:00 pm: Go to bed

Next morning

6:00 am: Wake up fully rested and energized for your 9:00 am interview!

Bonus #8. Arrive Early On Your Interview Day

Simple Strategy

Job interviews are some of the most important meetings of your life. But you can't succeed in a job negotiation if you arrive (or zoom in) late. There's a huge difference, for instance, between arriving late for a class lecture and arriving late for a job interview. Arriving late or appearing unprofessional for an interview can lead to a situation where you're fighting an uphill battle during the entire process. To avoid this, arrive early. It may seem like common sense, but it's not always common practice. Aim to arrive not just five minutes, but ideally a half hour or hour early. This has several advantages. First, you'll have time to compose yourself. Second, you'll have time to review (yet again) what you want to say and how you want to say it. Third, arriving early will give you time to relax (maybe not fully, but more than if you arrived just a few minutes before the interview). Fourth, you'll have time to adjust to your surroundings. Fifth, it's possible that one of the people conducting the interview will notice that you arrived early, which will set a positive tone for your interview. Last but not least, when waiting, always assume you're being watched. Treat everyone very well at every level. What goes around comes around. It's career karma.

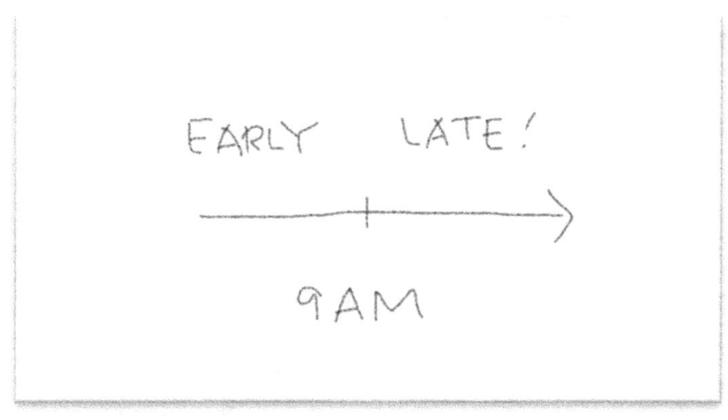

Simple Example

Your Arrival Time: 8:30am

Interview Time: 9:00am

Bonus #9. Choose Minimalist Zoom Backgrounds

Simple Strategy

Your Zoom (or similar online meeting app) background represents another dimension in your job interview's chessboard strategy. Most people don't give it too much thought. But your background represents a form of subtle, nonverbal communication strategy that can make or break your first impression. When choosing a background, professionalism, clarity and a distraction-free environment are key. One way to maximize the potential for a positive first impression is to choose a subtle, natural background — like a bookcase with several books or a plant — each can add warmth and personality without being overly distracting. Ensure the lighting is good and avoid cluttered areas. Another background option is using neutral colors like navy blue, gray, or beige, which are safe choices that project professionalism and calmness. Avoid bright or neon colors that can be distracting, unless it's subtle. If you decide to opt for virtual backgrounds, professional virtual backgrounds depicting a minimalist office environment or a clean, uncluttered room are often good choices. Make sure your virtual background is high-quality and free from glitches or large logos. Things to avoid are busy or cluttered backgrounds, unprofessional backgrounds, poorly lit backgrounds, overly personal backgrounds or brand-specific backgrounds. These can detract the attention *away* from you, rather than have them focus *on* you — and your qualifications for the job to get your worth.

Simple Example

Background themes

* A natural background with a subtle plant or bookcase

* A solid, neutral color background

* A high-quality virtual background of a minimalist office

* A clean and uncluttered room with good lighting

Bonus #10. Practice! Practice!! Practice!!!

Simple Strategy

We've all heard the mantra, "Practice makes perfect." At the same time, you must also know that the enemy of good is perfect. There's no such thing as perfect in the real world. Perfection only exists in theory. But know this: the goal of a job negotiation, or any negotiation, is not perfection, but *progress*. The more you do something, the better you become. Think of the first time you rode a bike or started swimming. Repetition, if done intentionally, reaps rewards. The key then is to do as many mock job interviews as possible. Give your cover letter and resume (CV), even if just draft versions, to a friend, family member, peers or all of the above for their honest and specific feedback. Write a list of possible questions you may be asked and write out (just don't think of) a script of possible answers. These scripts are not written in cement, they're just practice versions that can continually be updated and improved on over time. As a side note, a person's fear of job negotiations is often predicated on the unknown. So, repetition — let's call it *reps* — helps convert unknowns into knowns. This leads to greater confidence. And confidence is the precipice to success to get your worth.

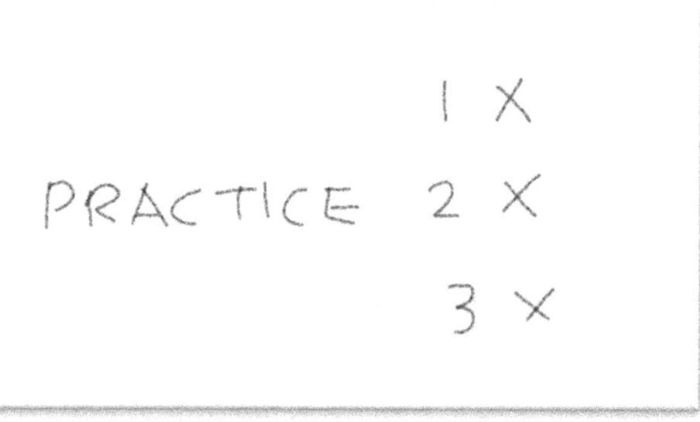

Simple Example

Sample List of Possible Job Interview Questions — To Practice, Practice, Practice!

Q: Tell me about yourself?
A: Write your answer to practice

Q: What makes you suited for this job?
A: Write your answer to practice

Q: What's your greatest weaknesses? Greatest strengths?
A: Write your answer to practice

Q: Describe a time when you failed? What did you learn from it?
A: Write your answer to practice

Q: When was the last time you changed your mind on an important topic?

A: Write your answer to practice

Q: What book, class or concept proved most instrumental to your current thinking?
A: Write your answer to practice

Q: How would you estimate the number of tennis balls that could fit into this room?
A: Write your answer to practice

References

Part 1

1. Know Your Breaking Point
Russell Korobkin, Aspirations and Settlement, 88 Cornell Law Review, Volume 1 (2002-2003)

2. Know Your Ideal Deal
Russell Korobkin, Aspirations and Settlement, 88 Cornell Law Review, Volume 1 (2002-2003)

3. What'S Your Yes Zone?
Russell Korobkin, Aspirations and Settlement, 88 Cornell Law Review, Volume 1 (2002-2003)

4. Should You Cooperate Or Compete?
Robert Axelrod and William D. Hamilton, The Evolution of Cooperation, Science, Volume 211, Number 4489 (1981)

5. Fight For Your Value
The Value of Customer Data by McKinsey & Company (2020), Data as a Competitive Advantage: How to Unleash the Power of Data and Analytics by Accenture (2023)

6. Likable Using Similarities
Brian Collisson and Jennifer L. Howell, The Liking-Similarity Effect: Perceptions of Similarity as a Function of Liking, The Journal of Social Psychology, Volume 154, Issue 5 (2014)

7. When To Frame As A Gain
Daniel Kahneman, Thinking, Fast and Slow, Farrar, Straus and Giroux (2011)

8. When To Frame As A Loss
Daniel Kahneman, Thinking, Fast and Slow, Farrar, Straus and Giroux (2011)

9. Using The Positivity Principle
Konstantina Prassa, Christos Pezirkianidis and Anastassios Stalikas, Investing the Role of Positive Emotions in Bilateral Negotiations: A Pilot Study, Psychology, Volume 13, Number 8 (2022)

10. Anchor Away
A.D. Galinsky and T. Mussweiler, First offers as anchors: The role of perspective-taking and negotiator focus, Journal of Personality and Social Psychology, Volume 81, Issue 4 (2001)

11. Find Your Why
Roger Fisher, William Dry and Bruce Patton, Getting to Yes: Negotiating Agreement Without Giving In, Penguin Books (2011)

12. Use Emotional Iq
Lauren A. Rivera, Go with Your Gut: Emotion and Evaluation in Job Interviews, American Journal of Sociology, Volume 120, Number 5 (2015)

13. Your Elevator Pitch Should Be Pitch Perfect
Nancy Duarte, HBR Guide to Persuasive Presentations, Harvard Business Review Press (2012)

14. Use Specific Words (From The Job Description)
Jennifer Herrity, How To Tailor Your Resume To A Job Description, Indeed, July 7 (2023)

15. Show Your Uniqueness
Indeed Editorial Team, Listing Hobbies and Interests on your Resume, Indeed, September 25 (2023)

16. If You've Got It, Flaunt It
Shana Lebowitz and Melia Robinson, The 'Power Poses' That Will Instantly Boost Your Confidence Levels, Inc., December 22 (2015)

17. Showcase Your Professional Skills
Eric Wargo, How Many Seconds to a First Impression? Association for Psychological Science, July 1 (2006)

18. Stay With Your Strengths
Ash All and Hasan Kubba, The Unfair Advantage: How Startup Success Starts With You, Profile Books (2020)

19. Strike A (Power) Pose
Shana Lebowitz and Melia Robinson, The 'Power Poses' That Will Instantly Boost Your Confidence Levels, Inc., December 22 (2015)

24. Forming First Impressions
Eric Wargo, *How Many Seconds to a First Impression? Association for Psychological Science*, July 1 (2006)

26. Find Your Unfair Advantage
Ash All and Hasan Kubba, *The Unfair Advantage: How Startup Success Starts With You, Profile Books* (2020)

27. Know Thyself (Self-Swot Analysis)
Lon Addams and Anthony T. Alfred, *The First Step in Proactively Managing Students 'Careers: Teaching Self-SWOT Analysis, Academy of Educational Leadership Journal*, Volume 17, Issue 4 (2013)

29. Evaluate Your 3e'S (Ethics, Emotions And Economics)
Jasper Kim, *Persuasion: The Hidden Forces That Influence Negotiations, Routledge Press* (2018)

32. Pursue Your 3p'S (Purpose, Passion, Profit)
Holly Tucker, *Do What You Love, Love What You Do, Random House*, May 6 (2021)

33. Feedback Is Fabulous
Mark Granovelter, *Getting a Job: A Study of Contacts and Careers, University of Chicago Press*, June 29 (2018)

34. Be A Bullet Point Bargainer
Don Descy, *Behind The Bullet Points: The Surprising Secrets of Powerful Presentations, Independently Published*, December 18 (2020)

37. Mindfully Meditate With Mozart
Frances H. Rauscher, Gordon L. Shaw and Catherine N. Ky, *Music and Spatial Task Performance, Nature*, Volume 365, Page 611 (1993)

39. Envision A Typical Day
Jasper Kim, *24 Hours with 24 Lawyers: Profiles of Traditional and Non-Traditional Careers, Thomson Reuters / West Publishing* (2011).

40. Investigate Your Interviewers
Richard Shell, *Bargaining for Advantage: Negotiation Strategies for Reasonable People, Penguin Books* (2006)

41. Walking Out Is A Strategy

Michelle Martín-Raugh, *Nonverbal Cues in the Employment Interview*, SPSP, December 26 (2022)

68. Use Positive Words (So You Appear More Positive)
Intelligent Change Staff, *The Benefits of Positive Language*, Intelligent Change (no date provided)

69. Splitting The Difference (Is Splitting Your Worth)
Chris Voss and Dahl Raz, *Never Split the Difference: Negotiating as if Your Life Depended on It*, Harper Business (2016)

72. Avoid (Excessive) Apologies
Anisa Purbasari Norton, *How To Stop Yourself From Saying 'Sorry 'All The Time*, Fast Company, January 15 (2018)

73. Concise Is Nice
Marty Nemko, *Verbosity: An Under-considered Contributor to Career and Personal Failure*, LinkedIn, August 20 (2018)

76. Dealing With Dirty Tactics
Katie Shonk, *Deceptive Tactics in Negotiation: How to Ward Them Off*, Program on Negotiation, January 15 (2024)

77. Leverage Logrolling
PON Staff, *Negotiations and Logrolling: Discover Opportunities to Generate Mutual Gains*, Program on Negotiation, March 4 (2024)

78. Silence Is A Wordless Weapon
Selena Razvani, *Speak Less, Win More: The Art of Silence in Negotiations at Work*, MSNBC, October 11 (2023)

79. What If I'M Insulted?
Michael Wheeler, *The Art of Negotiation: How to Improvize Agreement in a Chaotic World*, Simon & Schuster (2013)

80. Create Confidence By Curated Communication
Matt Abrahams, *Think Faster, Talk Smarter: How to Speak Successfully When You're Put on the Spot*, Simon Element (2023)

82. Flip The Tables (With Role Reversal)

About The Author

Dr. Jasper Kim offers expert insider secrets of success for negotiations, money and contracting. He has been featured on CNBC, CNN and Forbes. As a Wall Street banker and lawyer at global financial institutions like Barclays Capital and Credit Suisse, and academic affiliations with Harvard Law School and Oxford University. He lives with his family and rescue dog in California. Learn more at www.jasperkim.com.

Other Books by Dr. Jasper Kim

- *Persuasion: The Hidden Forces That Influence Negotiations*

- *24 Hours with 24 Lawyers: Profiles of Traditional and Non-Traditional Careers*

- *American Law 101: An Easy Primer on the U.S. Legal System*

- *Korean Business Law: The Legal Landscape and Beyond*

- *ABA Fundamentals: International Economic Systems*